3 1994 00950 1856

SANTA ANA PUBLIC LIBRARY

D1008259

*Praise for Molly Fumia's*
# HONOR THY CHILDREN

"[A] story that will break your heart and make it whole again. It will bring you into realms of humanness and compassion you didn't know you had. It might even set you free to love in ways you've never loved before." —*Sister Helen Prejean, author of* Dead Man Walking

"*Honor Thy Children* makes the unimaginable compelling, healing, and transformational." —*Melody Beattie, author of* Journey to the Heart

"A vital message . . . traces [the Nakatani's] ordeal with graceful compassion and delicacy, demonstrates that wholeness and healing can be achieved under what seem like impossible circumstances, and that love, trust and acceptance are necessary in every family." —*San Francisco Chronicle*


*Praise for Molly Fumia's* SAFE PASSAGE

"Is there a remedy to grief? Molly Fumia's moving words are indeed helpful—they are both inspired and inspiring." —*Elie Wiesel*

"[A] guide through the passages of grief—indeed, through the mysteries of life and death themselves—toward healing and hope." —*Sue Monk Kidd, author of* When the Heart Waits

"*Safe Passage* is the most sensitive heart healer for those who are going through loss." —*Gerry Jampolsky, author of* Love Is Letting Go of Fear

MOLLY FUMIA

Foreword by Ann Dunnewold, Ph.D.

# A PIECE *of* MY HEART

Living Through

the Grief of

Miscarriage,

Stillbirth, or

Infant Death

CONARI PRESS
Berkeley, California

155.937 FUM
Fumia, Molly
A piece of my heart

$14.95
NEWHOPE        31994009501856

Copyright © 2000 by Molly Fumia

All Rights Reserved. No part of this book may be used or reproduced in any manner whatsoever without written permission, except in the case of brief quotations in critical articles or reviews. For information, contact: Conari Press, 2550 Ninth Street, Suite 101, Berkeley, California 94710-2551.

Conari Press books are distributed by Publishers Group West.

Cover Photography: ©1999 Richard Pelletier/Tony Stone Images
Cover and book design: Claudia Smelser
Cover Art Direction: Ame Beanland

Library of Congress Cataloging-in-Publication Data

Fumia, Molly
   A piece of my heart : living through the grief of miscarriage, stillbirth, or infant death/ Molly Fumia ; foreword by Ann Dunnewold
   p.   cm.
Includes bibliographical references.
ISBN: 1-57324-510-0
1. Grief. 2. Bereavement—Pyschological aspects. 3. Infants (Newborn)—Death—Psychological aspects. 4. Miscarriage—Psychological aspects. 5. Fetal death—Psychological aspects. 6. Stillbirth—Psychological aspects. 7. Loss (Psychology) I. Title.
BF575.G7 F85 2000
155.9'37–dc21                                                    00–020656

Printed in the United States of America
00 01 02 03 MALLOY 10 9 8 7 6 5 4 3 2 1

*For Chuck*

# A Piece of My Heart

# Foreword

by Ann Dunnewold, Ph.D
author of *Postpartum Survival Guide*

As human beings, we anticipate parenthood with the hope that all will be well. Not just well, but perfect. We envision the healthy, happy, beautiful baby that we see in parenting magazines. Pregnancy and birth will be the fulfillment of that dream. "This will be the most wonderful time of my life," we wholeheartedly believe. As we anticipate parenthood, to have a baby die is unfathomable. Certainly we expect to be outlived by our children, to see our children have children and even grandchildren. Babies are not supposed to die. Yet approximately 1.1 percent of all babies die within the first year of life, according to the National Center for Health Statistics. Around

1 percent are stillborn, and another 10 to 14 percent of known pregnancies end in miscarriage.

Health professionals once believed that the most helpful strategy when dealing with parents who had lost a child was to minimize the developing bond between parent and child. "It is best this way," "The baby would not have been right," and similar platitudes were common consolations offered to grieving parents. The goal was to help the parents focus on the "positive," and thus to separate. This belief stemmed from early work in psychology, which hypothesized that grief was resolved when surviving loved ones "forgot" the one who had died, breaking the attachment. Unfortunately, Molly Fumia had her first son, Jeremy John, when this practice was still widespread. Now we know that parents have an easier time resolving their grief when given a chance to connect with, care for, and express love for their child. Remembering the infant, continuing the bond, and integrating the memories into your ongoing life is the way to heal. As Molly says, "Survival meant never to forget."

Despite the enlightenment of many health professionals to the natural grieving process, the fact remains that it is difficult to be with someone in grief. Whether trained professionals, loving friends, or family members, we all struggle with allowing a grieving person to feel their feelings. It is hard to watch a loved one in pain. Our natural tendency is to want to "make it better," by erasing the sadness. This bias is exaggerated in the death of an infant, full-term or younger. Unrealistic societal expectations persist: "A miscarriage is not yet a baby," "It is good that the loss came early, you were not yet bonded," or "You will have other children." Well-meaning people try to comfort the parents by minimizing the loss, attempting to protect them from anguish. Few of us know truly how to help others experience grief so that they can move through it. We let the bereaved parent hide from these overwhelming feelings, because encouraging numbness is safer, less challenging than facing the pain with them. Even when our intentions are good and we want to help a loved one confront their hurt and loss, we lack tools to do this. No one is teaching Grief 101 in high school.

Just as we are ill prepared to support our loved ones through the grieving process, we are even less skilled in recovering from our own devastating losses. New parents are susceptible to the myths about pregnancy loss and infantile death too, and often wonder "What is the matter with me for feeling so badly—I barely knew this baby?" or "I must be weak for feeling this so strongly."

*A Piece of My Heart* is an invaluable resource for this basic human problem: that we want to brush off the hurt and make the pain disappear. As Molly illustrates here, recovery does not work that way. She offers instruction in the process, the spiritual and emotional journey, which constitutes healing. This book instills hope that you can feel better by confronting the pain, not dismissing it. With her heartfelt descriptions, Molly provides validation of the grieving parent's experience. Her feelings are so true, so normal, as they bubble up around her, threatening to take over her life. It is very human to have emotions come from nowhere when you are grieving. Reminders of your loss are all around you, regularly triggering the sadness and anger you may have thought were resolved.

Crucial and effective strategies for recovery are presented in the final chapter. Molly urges you to honor the grief process, including your right to have your pain and feel it in order to be healed. Do not forget the undeniable mother-child bond, she asserts, including making the child real by using his or her name. She gives permission to remember the past, however long ago. Finally, know that there are others who know how you feel, and sharing your grief is a step to empowerment and healing. *A Piece of My Heart* clearly shows the way to grief recovery, whether the loss involves a child or other loved one. This book should be required reading for anyone who has experienced the death of a loved one or encounters those who need to grieve. In other words, all of us can benefit from the wise words in this book.

While the bereaved person's tendency is to avoid the pain, Molly suggests that we "imagine the pain to be a reminder only of my capacity for love." You may disbelieve, as you are immersed in your anguish, that good can come from this suffering. Indeed, the idea that to move through the pain will make you feel better may sound Pollyanna-ish, or dismissive, or unattainable. You may find that the horror of Molly's experience and of Elie Wiesel's recollections serves to increase your pain. Focus on the hope contained here, not just the loss. Do not take the solutions offered as literally the only way to heal, but use them as a model, trying on what works for you. Everyone is an individual, and Molly's path can serve as a guide for you. You must find your own path to healing, but the healing still can only come through the feelings, not by detouring around them. If the journey seems too overwhelming and painful on your own, search out a grief group and/or professional helper as partner in your pain. Finally, trust your own inner wisdom about what works for you, and what you need to move through the grief into compassion, both for yourself and others.

# A Question
# Mark

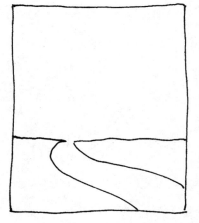

*"What is the death of a child?" Pedro asked.*

*"An injustice," I answered.*

*"No. That would be making a moral problem out of it.*
*It's more. It's a question mark."*

—Elie Wiesel, *The Town Beyond the Wall*

This is the story of what happened when Jeremy died . . . and a question mark was born. It is also the story of what happened when I found a friend with an explanation, and of the time in between, when the jagged edges of confusion, denial, and sorrow still threatened me.

I did not expect to become a storyteller. And I struggled with how my friend, whose name is Elie Wiesel, would feel about my devoting so much attention to my story when seen in light of his. Here is a person, I often thought, who not only witnessed the murders of most of his family and the people of his village, but has, through the burden of memory, insisted upon witnessing the murders of six million other human beings, a million and a half of them children.

From the beginning, it seemed to me that my suffering was so small in comparison. In my imagination, I confided to Elie Wiesel this hesitation. Who am I to compare a single, tragic experience to the loss of all hope and all humanity? In my imagination he smiled slightly, a bit frustrated, and pushed back the hair that flops on his forehead. And I understood that he would speak not of comparisons, but of connections: To remember the past is to be more alive, more human in the present. To connect one's personal human experience, one's singular sufferings, with all human experience, all suffering— it is then, he might say, that we in our humanness will begin to re-create the universe.

And so I found myself committed to a bold act. I used one story to tell another. I found a familiar ghost among his dead. I assumed that Elie wouldn't mind that I borrowed his memory of the six million, of the one and a half million children, to help me recall just one infant boy. Finally, despite my hesitation, I welcomed these unexpected truths: that I had a right and a need to mourn, that my feelings were honorable and important, and that I was not alone in my agony but joined by enough tiny, unlived lives and grieving parents to fill the heavens ten times over.

And so I offer my story to acknowledge, and bless, our common mourning. If I learned nothing else from my struggle, it is that grief is meant to be shared. To bring our sorrows to the embrace of another is to make of them allies rather than enemies. Not everyone who has experienced the death of an infant, a stillborn birth, or a miscarriage will find it necessary to travel all the roads I traveled in order to be whole again, but inevitably there will be some common ground. And it is in the sharing that we begin to be healed—and even empowered. It is my hope that the story of my hard-fought understanding might resound in your wounded spirit, as the memories and wisdom of the rebbe Elie Wiesel did in mine.

Admittedly, I am anxious to tell the ending of the tale. But it is important to begin at the beginning—to call forth the past. Sometimes, when the past has eluded our acceptance and hidden itself well in the shadows of memory, it resists mightily any call to consciousness. But when we somehow summon the strength to demand its presence, it bursts forth with a clarity and fullness that is astonishing, as if it had been waiting there, untouched, to be read in detail like frames of a film.

Therefore my story begins like that of my friend, dragged from memory to consciousness and told as precisely as possible. Then, once the words have been spoken, the story moves from memory to meaning. Along the way, I have interwoven Elie's words and borrowed a powerful literary device—a dialogue that transcends the actual events. In this way his words helped bring forth mine, as it should be between storytellers.

I did not expect to give myself away, to Elie Wiesel or anyone else. That I could be so influenced by the wisdom and experience of another was a startling self-admission. But in the end, it was I who was transformed by the giving over.

Even after all this time, I am still moved, deeply moved, by all that has happened. To say that I am thankful for this journey might never be enough. But it will have to do.

# The Story

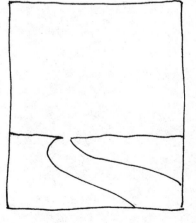

# Before the
# Death of
# Childhood

*The tale the beggar tells must be told from the beginning.*
*But the beginning has its own tale, its own secret.*

—Elie Wiesel, *A Beggar in Jerusalem*

Whenever I remind Charles that he declared his love for me on our first date, he doesn't remember it. How could anyone forget something like that? I remember. We had driven up to San Francisco. There we were, walking along the street, looking for where we had parked the car. He turned to me and said, "I love you." Just like that. And even though the setting was perfect for such a pronouncement, I didn't think it was romantic at the time. I thought it was pushy.

One time when we were laughing and arguing about that night, Charles insisted that I must have said that I loved him too. But I didn't say it—then. It was almost a year later, and again we were in San Francisco, up on Nob Hill in a little park between Grace Cathedral and the Fairmont Hotel. We were swinging back and forth on a set of swings, and I told him that I loved him. From then on, our choice for one another was easy, and for me, an event that fearlessly opened up the future to whatever might come along. My fortunes began with Charles, as did my plunge into the very real complexities of adulthood.

At the time, however, my joy over our relationship was uncomplicated and expectant. He was, and still is, a very handsome man. He has the olive skin of his Sicilian ancestors, thick, dark hair, and large, brown, expressive eyes that always look a little sad. Even before we decided to get married, I thought about how beautiful his children might be.

Just as Charles can't seem to recall our first date just as it happened, he also denies having discussed the idea of our having five children. But I remember. We were sitting outside a Chinese restaurant in San Jose. He said that his Aunt Maxine and Uncle Bob had five children, and he thought that was "about right." I was thrilled. I wanted lots of children, a large family like the one in my childhood fantasies.

As an only child, I spent many hours daydreaming about what it would be like to have more people around. I already had an extra bed, intended, I was sure, for a little sister. When I was very small, I lived with two imaginary friends. A little later on, I drafted plans for huge families living wonderfully together in sprawling houses where I shared the best bedroom with one of my many beloved siblings. Eventually, I was embarrassed by my secret imaginings, and I turned to the occasional friend who was allowed to spend the night to fill the empty bed, moved close to mine, and share the whispered intimacies I believed to be the domain of real sisters.

But no one could come to my house on special nights—like Christmas Eve. It was such a silly thought, spending Christmas Eve with a friend, but I imagined it anyway. Waiting for Christmas morning with a houseful of brothers and sisters was one of my favorite fantasies.

A month after the movie in San Francisco and his declaration of love, Charles invited me to his family's Christmas Eve gathering. I couldn't believe I had a date to Christmas. My parents couldn't believe it either.

Charles' entire family—grandparents, aunts and uncles, cousins, as well as his parents, his two sisters and their families, and his little brother—welcomed me and the other "dates" (Charles has lots of cousins) as if we had always been part of the group. They were very lively and quite direct, as I caught snatches of arguments and confrontations going on as naturally as the warm Christmas greetings they were sharing. I wondered if this was the way big families were, so robust and unrestrained.

We got married on June 26, 1971, exactly one week after I graduated from college. Our family and friends toasted to our good health and to our many children-to-be. We raised our glasses while everyone cheered. I remember thinking, Is that what comes next . . . our many children? Suddenly bestowed on me was the blessing and authority to create the family I had always imagined. I looked around at our closest friends. Nancy and Gerry had been married for a year and were anxious to start a family. Donna and Robert had been married two years longer, and were beginning to worry about the fact that they hadn't yet conceived a child. And Terry and Rick, whose wedding we would celebrate late that summer, were laughing about how Terry might follow in her mother's footsteps and become pregnant quickly and often. Apparently, the path before all of us had been happily determined.

Our friends and family toasted us, again and again, sending us on our way. At the time, it seemed so simple. The future was taken care of; the past could be abandoned easily. We were swirling around inside today, and it was, for the moment, glorious.

🙦 🙦

Charles and I returned from a month-long trip to Europe and rented an old, comfortable apartment not far from the college. On the day we moved in, we were greeted with an endless array of boxes and, to our surprise, Robert and Donna, who lived in an apartment below us. So during those first few hectic months, when Charles was settling into his job with the family ranching business and I was back in college pursuing a teaching credential, we could share our new life together with others who seemed to be just a little ahead of us.

Donna was deeply concerned about not being pregnant. She and Robert were talking about taking some tests that sounded, at best, unpleasant. As for me, although having a child was not in my immediate plans, neither had I ruled out the possibility. Donna's fears unnerved me. Would we have similar troubles? How soon should we start trying, if only to prove that we were capable of becoming parents? The implications of success were only fleetingly considered.

Meanwhile, Nancy and Gerry announced that their waiting was over. The telling seemed like half the fun; their first child was due in September. Gerry was pleased, but Nancy was, indeed, radiant. Suddenly her future was full of meaning, and she was completely ready for the baby's arrival within a few weeks of discovering she was pregnant. I couldn't help but share in her exuberance and decide, sometime during those days, that I dearly wanted to have something just as exciting to tell and to feel those wonderful feelings too.

Our unspoken ambivalence toward family planning quickly paid off. In March 1972, nine months after our wedding, Charles and I discovered that we were going to have a baby. Of course, by then, it seemed like a great idea. The family was excited, the grandparents ecstatic. It was fun to be pregnant: new clothes, new expectations, a name to choose, a room to ready. We moved into a small old house in downtown San Jose, and after finishing my teaching program in June, I settled down to a summer of waiting.

We went to childbirth classes where I learned to breathe deeply and Charles learned how to nod and say, "You're doing fine." Still, I was afraid of the event. But then Nancy had her baby—a little boy they named Gregory—and seemed to survive the pain we had worried about many times together. There was my baby shower, where Nancy brought Gregory, who stole the show from the expectant mother. I wished that I had been first to deliver. Nancy was already thin and back to business as usual.

The baby was due on Halloween. I had thought that was a little odd, but of no real significance to our child. As the time drew nearer, I felt the glow of pregnancy disappear. My body strained to accommodate a large and active baby. I remember telling Charles that there were no words to adequately describe the last weeks of pregnancy. And I still had the delivery to look forward to.

October 31 came and went. I stayed up all night waiting for Pasha, our German Shepherd, to have her puppies. She worked very hard, but by morning she had delivered only two. Just before noon I phoned Charles—two more had arrived. By the time Charles came home that evening, there were eleven. At ten o'clock that night she delivered her last puppy, a stillborn male. I held him in my hand and observed his perfect features: He looked just like his brothers and sisters. Pasha had been too tired to push him through the birth canal quickly, and he had probably suffocated there while she struggled to bring him into the world. Pasha lifted her head and watched me while I wrapped up her puppy in a towel and carried him away. When I came back, she nudged me gently and gave a little whine.

"It's okay, Pasha," I told her, "you've got enough babies." She seemed to contemplate my words, and then, exhausted, she put her head back down. I envied her. It was over and she could rest.

Two more weeks went by. The puppies grew and thrived, but I was losing interest in any babies other than my own. In spite of the familiar terror, I felt ready. This I remember, that all concerns about pain were overwhelmed by impatience. I was ready to have a child, at any cost.

# Remembering
# the Week

*He burrowed in his memory, and searched carefully.*
*He turned pages, weighed episodes, examined the faces*
*buried pell-mell in his depths. Finally he knew, from the*
*trembling of his heart, that he had found what he wanted.*

—Elie Wiesel, *The Town Beyond the Wall*

O n the night of November 11, while celebrating our neighbor and dear friend Robert's birthday, I went into labor. I felt as though we were finally performing our parts in the play, after months of rehearsal. There were lots of laughing and worried looks, especially from the men, as I calmly finished my piece of birthday cake while everyone else timed my contractions. Charles' anxiety got us to the front door eventually, and after saying a hurried good-bye to the roomful of friends, we went home to pick up my long-packed suitcase, and to make sure that this was the real thing.

It was. My water broke as we walked into the house; the contractions speeded up and intensified. Nevertheless, when we arrived at the hospital we were informed that we had a long night ahead of us.

I slept on and off as the hours wore on. Next door to me, a young Mexican girl screamed periodically in Spanish. A nurse came by and tried in vain to comfort her. She looked at me and rolled her eyes, her annoyance evident. I decided that I would not scream, no matter how much it hurt, so that the nurses would not talk about me to the other patients.

Finally, at about six in the morning, I began to progress. The nurses were full of praise—how brave I had been, how easy my delivery would be. I was pleased. This was working out just fine.

Both my doctor and his partner were off duty for the weekend, and another doctor whom I had never seen before came to say he would be delivering our baby. Dr. Simpson seemed nice enough, though a bit distant, and probably sleepy. He had been waiting for me all night. I felt badly about that.

The nurse came in with good news. I was ready for a caudal, an anesthesia that numbs the body from the waist down. While we waited for it to be administered, Charles and I congratulated each other on the ease with which we had met this challenge. I had done a great job; he had been a wonderful coach. And now it was almost over. I wondered what the baby would be like. The caudal was given, and the intense pain, which I had been controlling with the breathing exercises learned in class, slowly diminished to nothing. A nurse came in. She could see the baby's head; I was ready.

Once in delivery, I chatted with everyone, free of pain, feeling proud and excited, cooperating as much as I could. Charles came in dressed from head to toe in hospital garb. Underneath the surgical mask, I knew he was smiling.

The baby, a boy, arrived at 8:12 A.M., Sunday, November 12, 1972. Charles and I cried when our son cried for the first time. I held him for a moment, then the nurses insisted that he be taken away to be cleaned up and weighed. I fell asleep on and off while Dr. Simpson finished his post-delivery work. Someone came back with the news that the baby weighed 8 pounds, 15 ounces.

"No wonder I have so much sewing to do," the doctor said. He looked up at me. "What's the baby's name?"

"Jeremy John Fumia," I said firmly. I love that name.

When I arrived in my room in the maternity ward several hours later, the numbness had begun to wear off and with it my good spirits.

"It's your first and he was big. It's to be expected," the nurse attending to me explained.

The pain got worse and worse, and I felt that if I moved I would surely break in two. My head began to ache—a side effect of the caudal.

Charles came in with reports on how the news had been received by our families. Would I like to be the one to call our friends, Nancy and Gerry, or maybe Robert and Donna? I managed one phone call, but did not enjoy the telling. Charles brought gifts, but they diverted my attention only momentarily. Where was my baby?

Finally, at about eight o'clock, twelve hours after delivery, a nurse brought him to me. I sat up painfully, but willingly, and reached for him. The nurse regarded me with a hint of exasperation.

"This is your first? Well, we have a procedure."

One little foot protruded from the tightly wrapped blanket around the baby and on it was a hospital bracelet.

"These numbers much match," she demanded, grabbing my wristband. When they did, she laid him on a sterile pad on the bed and undressed him for me.

I followed this activity with interest, nodding and murmuring my recognition of the fact that all of his parts seemed to be in order, flawless. I wondered if he was cold. It was, after all, November. She rearranged his little diaper and shirt and wrapped him back up.

"Watch out when you change his diaper. Little girls dribble, but little boys squirt." I grinned, not having thought of that.

"I see that you're bottle-feeding." She frowned—or was that my imagination? "Well, he might not take too much. Put him up on your shoulder and burp him after an ounce."

She handed the baby to me, and I responded with awkwardness. I tried to act naturally, making cooing noises at Jeremy while waiting for her to leave. But she was busy raising up the metal sides of my bed. She probably thinks I'll drop him, I reflected. Finally, we were alone. He wasn't too interested in eating and seemed quite drowsy. We sat there together, but still separate. Maybe I should talk to him, I thought. Once when his eyes were open, I hoped that he was looking at me, despite what I had heard about babies not being able to focus for several weeks.

"Hello, Jeremy," I said, and then added, "Hello, Jeremy John."

He fell asleep and I put the bottle down beside me, hardly touched. I looked at my son. His skin was olive, his hair brown. He had a cute little upper lip that poked out over a definite chin. Gently I took his hand. His fingers were long like mine. Piano fingers, my mother had called them. They moved a little as he slept.

After a while I noticed I was no longer concentrating on him. The pain of sitting up was almost too much to bear. Where is the nurse, I wondered, vaguely aware of the quiet and loving conversation that was going on between my room-mate and her two-day-old daughter. I looked down at my baby.

"Next time," I whispered to him, "we'll get to know each other."

Finally a nurse, a different one, came in to retrieve him.

"Did he eat?" she asked.

"Not really," I admitted, wondering if that was really okay.

"Don't worry," she smiled, aware of my insecurity. "Most of the time it takes them a while to get going."

They left, and I was reassured. He would eat next time. He would learn.

A nurse came in with painkillers. "Your doctor said you can have one of these every four hours." I felt protected. Everyone was taking care of me. "Do you want us to bring you your baby during the night? Or do you want to sleep?"

I wanted to sleep and escape the pain, but I didn't want to be a bad mother.

"You can bring him," I said.

"Then we'll see you at midnight."

I slept soundly until the nurse turned on my light and gave me a washcloth to clean my hands and a sterile pad for my lap.

"Babies are coming!" she crooned as she swept through the room. I heard her words being echoed down the hall.

Jeremy didn't eat at all. I gave up after a few feeble attempts to interest him in the bottle of formula. I kept dozing off, waking each time with a start. My son slept peacefully in my arms. When the nurse came, she woke both of us. I admitted that he had slept the entire time, and I asked for more painkillers.

"Would you like him at four?" My hesitation gave me away. "As long as you're bottle-feeding, maybe you should try to sleep until morning, dear," she said. "We usually feed the bottle-feds in the nursery during the night."

She had given me an out. I took it.

❧ ❧

*Monday morning.* Jeremy is one day old, I thought. I felt better, and I was anxious for him to come. When they brought him in, his eyes were open, and I decided to work hard at getting him to eat. He sucked a little bit, squirmed, even cried. I tried for what seemed like a very long time, becoming more and more uncomfortable. He didn't seem happy. Was he going to be a cranky baby?

"Come on, Jeremy," I said softly. "You have to eat." He didn't, and they took him away, leaving me alone behind the curtains that encircled the bed. I felt like crying, but didn't.

Later on, the baby's pediatrician came in. Steve Larussa was an old friend, my friend Nancy's father, and, of course, little Gregory's doctor, too.

"He looks fine, can't find a thing wrong with him," he reported in his familiar drawl. We chatted together about other things. I was glad to see Steve.

"He's not really eating yet," I confided, trying to sound casual and unconcerned.

"Give him time he'll be eating you out of house and home."

I nodded, again reassured by the sound of his voice, tinged with both affection and sarcasm. And I clung to that remark, predictable as it was, as if it was a prognosis rather than a cliché.

The day continued with many visitors and more gifts. I shuffled painfully to the nursery, flanked by all four grandparents. Their happiness flowed easily, blending into the conversations of other proud baby-watchers pressed close to the long viewing window.

"Look at that chin. He looks like his daddy."

"He looks just like Grandpa Fumia."

"He's beautiful, Molly, just beautiful."

Deep inside, a strong current of worry was beginning to thread its way through my entire being. I wasn't able to identify it; I only know that I wasn't as happy as I should be. I decided that once I started feeling better, everything would be all right.

When visiting hours ended, I was glad to be alone. I tried to write out birth announcements, but I stopped after two. I concentrated on the gifts, especially on a tiny football jersey with "Fumia" on the back that was hanging from the curtain rod around my bed. I tried to imagine my son wearing it, but the image was hazy. I turned on the television.

That evening Steve Larussa came by again.

"The baby has a little fever."

I shivered involuntarily, as if waking up too fast. I swallowed. "Is that bad?"

"Well, I don't like it. It's only a hundred and one. That's not very high. I told them to call me if it goes higher."

If it goes higher. . . "What could the fever be from?" In an instant, terrible answers went through my mind. Why can't everything be all right?

"Did you have a cold when you came in?"

My throat had been slightly sore during the past week, as if I had been fighting off a cold. Once in the hospital I had ignored it completely. I was suddenly uplifted by the possibility of an explanation.

"You know, I have been feeling like I'm coming down with something."

"Why don't you wear a surgical mask while you're feeding him? It's not good for an infant to be exposed to our infections."

So at the eight o'clock feeding, I wore a mask. While I waited for him arrive, I thought about our situation. An infection from me. He wasn't eating. He had a fever.

The nurse delivered my son to my arms. His eyes were wide open. I looked down at him. How long would I have to wear this mask? He probably wonders who I am. I felt like I couldn't communicate with him. I felt far away, less of a mother, more helpless.

I tried holding him in different positions, but none of them helped him want to eat. I was unhappy, nervous and self-conscious about the mask. There was nothing between the other babies and their mothers; it seemed like something big and unexplainable was between us.

The baby went back to the nursery. The tears finally came. I was frustrated, in pain, and worried. Charles called, understanding and reassuring, as always. The fever was probably nothing. Didn't I remember—the same thing had happened to a baby of some friends of ours. Everything would be all right. Some sleep might help my "baby blues."

I hung up the phone. Charles was right, of course. The fever was not unusual and probably not important. The mask was bearable if it would keep my son from further infection. I shouldn't allow the mask to make me feel this way. It was just a thin piece of material; everything else was just the same as with the other mothers. I drifted off to sleep.

When a nurse I hadn't seen before brought Jeremy at midnight, I woke up quickly. I put the mask on, feeling refreshed, knowing that there would be change. And he did seem hungrier. I kept holding up the bottle; he had taken an ounce! I put him up on my shoulder and patted his back. This is the way it will be, I thought. He will eat and I will pat his back. With his little head snuggling up to mine, I felt close and good. Daring further infection from my hand, I touched his forehead. He didn't feel warm. The fever was probably gone. Soon he dozed off, but I would have something report to the nurse.

"Did he eat?" she asked methodically.

"Yes, over an ounce."

"Good. He hasn't been eating too much in the nursery, but we figure he's so big, he doesn't need to eat yet."

Was this the time I kissed him on the forehead? I don't think so; I allowed the mask to keep me from him. Beneath it, I smiled as the nurse picked him up. She looked at my son, and he looked back.

"Were you a good boy and eat for Mommy?" Just like all the other babies. "Say good-bye to Mommy."

Was this the time I said, "Good-bye, Jeremy"? Was there a glance, an instant that we connected? Did he feel my hesitant, yet ever-growing love as we parted? The mask, the mask. He couldn't have seen my smile as I watched his little head disappear out of the room.

I would never hold him again.

Moments later, the nurse who had taken Jeremy away returned.

"We won't be bringing him at four. We don't usually bring the bottle-fed babies in the middle of the night. No need to."

An objection, so slight I hardly noticed it, raised itself softly. There was a need—my need—but that secret would remain unrevealed for years.

"And besides," she continued, not looking at me while she gave my pitcher of water a jiggle, "he has that fever."

I was disappointed, but I told myself the eating and the sleeping would help him . . . and me.

After nearly eight hours of sleep, I welcomed Tuesday morning with optimism. I lay awake listening to breakfast trays rattling and the clink of a mop against the furniture. An old woman was singing while she mopped my floor. Doctors came and went, talking and laughing with the mothers. The maternity ward is a happy place, I reflected to myself, different from the rest of the hospital.

A head came around the corner of my door. "It's your turn for a shower."

I stood for a long time enjoying the hot water on my bruised body. When I got back to my room, my bed was freshly made and a nurse was waiting for me.

"Will you be going home today?"

"Home?" This had not occurred to me. It seemed too soon. And besides, the baby had a fever. "I don't think so," I said, aware that I must have sounded meek and unmaternal. "My doctors haven't been in yet."

I got into bed and readied myself for the feeding. In the hall babies were whimpering. Was that Jeremy crying? He's probably hungry, I thought with a burst of confidence. My roommate had gone home; the next baby to come into my room would be mine. As footsteps came down the hall toward me, I sat expectantly.

It was Steve Larussa. He put his hands on his hips. "I think we'd better leave the baby in the nursery." My spirits plummeted. "That fever is persisting, and we don't want to take any chances."

No, we don't, I thought dismally. "When will we be able to go home?" I hadn't considered the possibility of leaving without him.

"We'll see. We have to get that fever down." He looked sad. "I'll keep you posted."

I tried not to listen to the other babies being reunited with their mothers. I began to ache all over. I asked for a painkiller.

I called Charles with the latest development. He didn't say much; he would be by after lunch. A new roommate arrived, fresh from the delivery room, and immediately I began to dread the moment her baby would arrive and mine wouldn't.

During visiting hours, Charles and I walked down to see him. He was off by himself, so as not to infect the other babies, I imagined. He was sleeping, a full bottle of water at the end of his little bed. Later, when visitors arrived, I took them down to see him in his lonely place at the end of the viewing window. Our friends and relatives didn't seem too concerned, or perhaps they were hiding their fears from me. Only my mother asked the questions that were rumbling around in my own heart.

"Well, what do they think it is, Molly? That doesn't seem right, a new little baby like that having a fever."

The whine in her voice annoyed me. "They don't know, Mother," I snapped. "They think he caught my cold."

She stood peering anxiously through the glass, indulging in concern. If she's going to get this upset, why doesn't she leave, I wondered cruelly. I turned away from her and walked back down the hall to my room.

The many trips to the nursery window took their toll. I couldn't wait for the painkillers to arrive at each four-hour interval. The babies came and went, and I sank into a stupor. I wanted the time to pass so that I would not have to feel anything.

A nurse came by to report. "The fever isn't too high, but we'll keep him in the nursery tonight." I didn't reply and turned back to the television.

Charles came to eat dinner with me. Afterward, I remember taking his arm and walking down to see our son that night. The nurses arranged to open the curtains for us. He was sleeping, with a little frown upon his face.

By the door of my room, Charles put his arms around me. "Everything's going to be all right," he said. I nodded into his shoulder. He took a step back and smiled. "When can I pick you up tomorrow?"

"I'll call you."

He left, and I took my painkillers and went to sleep.

🙡 🙡

*Wednesday.* A whole lifetime in just one day. After breakfast I waited to be checked out by a doctor. I tried to guess who would be coming. I had not seen Dr. Simpson, who delivered Jeremy, since Sunday afternoon. My own obstetrician, Dr. Kara, had come in only once, very briefly, on Tuesday. It seemed he was supposed to be on vacation.

Dr. Kara's partner, Dr. Mancini, came in about ten o'clock. He was much younger than Dr. Kara, who was white-haired, slightly built, and soft-spoken. Vince Mancini had dark unruly hair that rippled over his head and a pudgy stomach that, despite the best efforts of his belt, escaped over his pants and outside his suit coat. He was loud and friendly, taking over the room as he entered it.

"You're all set, Molly. Everything's fine. I've ordered more painkillers for you to take home with you. Any questions?"

I liked him. He sounded so sure. Perhaps he could take control of the situation.

"The baby had a fever yesterday," I said, "but I think we're still going home." It felt good to say that, and I wanted it to be true. Dr. Mancini only grinned as he scribbled something on my chart, and before he left he congratulated me heartily on my recent motherhood.

A nurse came by. "Going home today?"

"I hope so."

"I'll go check it out for you," she offered. I was thankful. I wanted to be sure.

An aide came in and helped me pack. The hospital "gifts" were put in a large plastic bag. We laid out Jeremy's going-home clothes, which had been chosen months ago. I got caught up in the preparations and momentarily forgot the physical discomfort and my worries. I called Charles, confident that everything was normal, just like the other mothers and babies I had watched routinely departing for a new life together.

"Bring an extra blanket for the baby and pick me up at eleven." How nice it felt to take care of my son. This is the way it would be always.

I waited for the nurse to return. When she didn't, I began to notice the soreness once again. It intensified quickly, and making a place among all of our belongings, I sank back down onto the bed. I closed my eyes for a moment and when I opened them again, a nun in full habit was standing at my door.

"Mrs. Fumia, this is for your baby boy." She handed me a tiny gold medal hanging from a blue ribbon.

I took the medal and looked up at her. She seemed quite pleased with herself.

"God bless you, dear," she whispered, and then she was gone.

I examined the gift. It was familiar enough, a medal commemorating the Immaculate Conception of Mary, the mother of Jesus. She was standing on a cloud in her long flowing robes, halo above her head, radiating goodness. The words around her were almost too tiny to read, but it didn't matter; they were probably stored somewhere in my memory.

"Mary conceived without sin, pray for us who have recourse to thee," I recited absently. Turning it over in my hand— pink for girls, I decided.

I thought about all the plastic statues and little medals I had received as a child for knowing my catechism lessons. I wondered where they were now. Perhaps up in a box in my mother's closet. Or maybe she threw them away.

The medal dangled from its ribbon in front of my eyes. Slowly I closed my hand around it, clutching it tightly. I could feel it coming. A long, silent wave of fear was pursuing me, then crushing me. A gift for Jeremy. The thought came and went without my holding it: *This is the only thing I will keep.*

Charles arrived and we waited. The nurse finally returned to inform us that Dr. Larussa was checking the baby out now and that she would bring him down as soon as he was finished. I nodded calmly, not wanting the normalcy of the moment to be cluttered with unnecessary words.

Finally, Steve arrived. One look at his face and panic came racing back. Up to the time, and since then, I have never known him to be so serious.

"I think we should leave the baby here another day. I want to have him checked out by another pediatrician."

We sat there, stunned. "Is the fever back?" I managed.

"The fever is low grade. I don't know what's causing it. If I let him go home, I'm afraid you'll just be right back in here." He hesitated. "I just don't feel good about this."

It all happened so quickly. With Steve's last words, the facade of normalcy that I had been holding up so vigilantly crumbled. I got a glimpse of what lay behind it—something new and terrifying. I don't remember lingering for very long, perched on the precipice of unknown, endless feelings. Instead, I thought about Steve's instincts, which seemed to point down a safer path.

And for years, I was grateful for the course he set for us. Since the baby didn't come home, I didn't get attached, I would say, and everyone would quietly agree. And the crib, and the clothes, and the stuffed dog we bought in Carmel just before he was born—what would I have done with all of that? They were never his. They would wait for the next baby. Everything would be all right. Much later, I wondered how I could have felt these things, and cursed Steve's instincts.

As we were leaving, a hospital volunteer came by with the customary birth photographs. The baby's head was tipped to one side, his eyes tightly closed, the fingers of one hand sprayed out awkwardly, as if the photographer had startled him. I felt like I didn't know this baby. I didn't buy the pictures.

Many times afterward I regretted that curious decision. When we tried to retrieve the photos nine years later, the negatives had recently been discarded.

I sat in the wheelchair, holding my suitcase instead of my newborn. A nurse wheeled me down the hall while Charles walked beside me, the blanket he brought for our baby on his arm. As we sat waiting for the elevator, I thought about going to see him through the nursery window before we left. He would be all alone, far away from the other babies. The effort seemed overwhelming; I didn't say anything to Charles or to the nurse. We stared at the elevator doors in a long silence.

I finally started to cry when my father greeted us at our front door. My mother stood waiting for us in the living room, which was immaculate, like the rest of the house she had prepared for our homecoming. In the middle of the floor was the cozy bassinet that our friend Esperanza had made. I noticed how nicely the bassinet sheet stretched across the little mattress; there was a diaper pad laid out where his head would be, in case he drooled, I supposed. Another diaper was draped over the side of the little bed, folded perfectly. Everything was perfect. Everything except our baby.

I hurt all over, and I lay down on the couch, which would be my place for many days. Through the tears, I could see my father looking at me. He didn't say anything. I turned to my mother, who was trying to smile in the face of disaster.

"They're probably just being cautious. He'll probably come home tomorrow," she said, and then added, "You want him to get well, don't you?"

If only my wanting could help. I wasn't so sure he would come home tomorrow. I wasn't sure at all that he would get well. For a long time I said that I had known from the beginning. I never say that anymore.

I took my painkillers and dozed on and off, worrying through the haze. Later in the afternoon Steve Larussa called. He and another pediatrician had determined that the baby's heart was enlarged. They didn't know exactly why. The baby would be moved by ambulance to the neonatal unit at Valley

Medical Center, where Dr. Carl Geraty, a pediatric cardiologist, could attend him. I could feel Jeremy traveling farther and farther away from me. I didn't try to hold on. We won't be picking him up at the hospital tomorrow, I mused. If we go, he won't be there.

By six o'clock that evening, our baby was at the new hospital. I couldn't imagine him there; it was a different place, unfamiliar. Eventually, I realized that I could no longer imagine him.

The new doctor called. His voice was very soft, and controlled.

"Mrs. Fumia, this is Dr. Geraty. I've just examined your baby." He took a little breath. "It doesn't look very good. We want to do some more tests."

He paused. I didn't say anything.

"I want to emphasize that this is very serious. You have a very, very sick baby."

I listened to the words. The baby was real. The baby was real and very, very sick.

"We want to do a cardiac catheterization. The baby has only a 50–50 chance of surviving this test." His voice continued to be soft and controlled. "We think we know what is wrong, and the test will confirm it. As I said, if it is what I think it is, it is very serious."

"Will you do the test tonight?"

"Immediately, but we need your okay. Your baby won't feel much of anything; he'll be sedated. He won't be in any greater danger than he is now, really, and at least we'll know for sure."

"Will you call us?"

"As soon as I can, I promise."

I reported the conversation to Charles and my parents. No one said anything.

An hour later, Carl Geraty called back. I was in our bedroom, sitting on the bed. Charles came in to sit next to me and put his ear to the phone I held between us. We listened to the doctor's already familiar voice.

"The baby survived the cardiac cath." He took another little breath. "I'm afraid our suspicions have been confirmed. "

"Yes?"

His voice rose as he lapsed into details and technical names. The baby had a congenital heart condition called hypoplastic left heart syndrome. The lower left ventricle was one-fifth the size it should be, and it contained only a few drops of blood. After he finished, I asked him what I needed to know.

"Are you telling us there's no hope?"

"Yes. It's terminal."

Beside me, Charles drew a sharp breath. Then for a moment there were no other sounds as the end of hope settled upon us and a new time of waiting began.

"How long does it usually take?" I asked finally. If I let go now, would it be too soon?

"Maybe a day, maybe a week, a month. The longest I've seen a baby with this condition survive is two months. This is only the second time I've seen it. It's actually very rare. Most common in firstborn boys."

For a blessed moment, my mind wandered. Our next one won't be the firstborn. Then I was jolted back to reality by the thought of two months of waiting. I hoped it wouldn't be that long. My immediate concern was that it be over quickly. How long would he be there, dying, while we waited?

The doctor continued. "Mrs. Fumia, I don't advise you coming down here. If it were my wife, I wouldn't allow her to come. There's really no point. There's nothing you can do."

My mind jumped. We had already been separated. *There's*

*nothing you can do. There's no point in coming. I wouldn't allow it.* His words would echo in my head all week.

I hadn't thought about going or not going. Suddenly, I realized he was making it easy for me.

"Like I said," he repeated with even more emphasis, as if he knew he had my attention, "if it were my wife, I wouldn't allow her to come."

"You wouldn't?" I pretended to be deciding. I didn't want to go. Somehow, I had already gotten through the letting go and now it was too late. Anyway, I shouldn't go—the doctor had advised against it. He would call us tomorrow. I put the receiver down and stared at it. That's odd, I thought. Just yesterday we were worried about his having a cold.

I walked back into the living room. "It's terminal," I said as I returned to my place on the couch. My mother, leaning against the door, uttered a little moan followed by deep, uncontrolled sobbing. My father moved to comfort her. Charles came and sat next to me and took my hand.

"I knew it," I declared. I was moving past the present a quickly as I could, running in slow motion, trying not to notice what was passing by.

There was nothing to do but sleep. As I approached our bed, I felt afraid. When I lay down in the silence and the stillness, would I have to think, would I have to feel? I took my pills. Charles and I held each other and I began to cry. Then it was morning.

🙦 🙦

*Thursday.* Charles' mother Catherine arrived early with rolls from the bakery around the corner. We talked a little and she said it wasn't meant to be, and I felt glad she was there. She would make this day somehow bearable.

I could hear her out in the kitchen, chatting with the dog. Pretty soon Pasha escaped into the living room and trotted over to see me on the couch.

"How's the mother?" I asked, stroking her head. She closed her eyes, happy for the attention. Only a few more weeks, I thought, and all the puppies will have gone to their new homes. Pasha will probably miss them.

I asked Catherine to take the dog back outside.

I thought of things to do. I became obsessed with the need to talk to my own doctor, Dr. Kara. I thought I should tell him what was happening. He would want to know. I got his home number from a mutual friend and left messages for him to call me. He finally called back later in the morning and listened quietly as I brought him up to date. He was very sorry. He would prescribe something for me; could someone pick it up? After we hung up, Catherine reminded me that he had recently lost a ten-year-old son, the youngest of his eight children, to cancer. I felt embarrassed. Maybe I shouldn't have bothered him at home. To lose a ten-year-old, compared to an infant that you barely know. . . .

As the day progressed, the family members were notified, and several of them called or came over. Dr. Geraty called. The baby was comfortable, he said, eating a little, being cared for in the best neonatal facility around. How was I? Had my doctor prescribed something for me? Yes, Charles would pick it up this afternoon.

It was decided that Charles would go with his father, Johnny, and sister, Janet, to see the baby that evening. I sat on the couch and took this news apprehensively. Should I go too? Charles said that I shouldn't go if I didn't feel up to it. Inside I hoped I would never feel up to it. If he were still alive next week, there wouldn't be a reason for me not to go. But Dr.

Geraty wouldn't allow his wife that pain. It must, indeed, be a terrible thing to see one's dying child. I took the pills that Charles brought home and more painkillers.

While Charles, Janet, and Johnny went to Valley Medical Center, I stayed on the couch and waited. Hazy images tumbled about my mind, without consideration, without my permission.

They are at the hospital by now. They are moving closer. Soon he will be there, in front of them. They will have to look.

Johnny will not be afraid. Many years ago, he watched his younger brother, Charles, while he was dying. Johnny looked into his face, too young for death, while he lay in his casket.

Even now Johnny grieves for his beloved brother. I wondered about that. In my life, I had never known a wound that didn't seem to heal, even a little. . . .

My mind slowed down and my body relaxed. I stared out the window at the trees in the front yard. It was dusk. Each small pane of glass was a perfect rectangle. The leaves on the trees were brown and yellow and red, and falling as I looked without seeing. Charles' blue Ford was parked in its usual place next to the curb. My eyes moved from the trees to the leaves to the black wrought iron railing next to the steps of our front porch and back to the trees. The bark on the biggest tree was uneven and chipping away like the paint on the house next door.

Across the room my mother and Catherine sat nervously on the loveseat. My mother had been going in and out of the kitchen, waiting for me to use a glass or a dish so that time could be spent washing it, drying it, and putting it away. Catherine had stayed in the living room, standing only a few feet away from me, looking through the basket of cards that we had received since Jeremy's birth. But now the dishes were done and all of the cards had been read. The scene seemed almost comical, the two of them, squeezed together on the loveseat while I stretched out on the long couch. Once in awhile, someone would say something, but I didn't really listen.

Suddenly my mother gave a little shriek and jumped up. She had burnt a hole in the loveseat with her cigarette. She apologized profusely and scurried about, trying to undo the hole, I imagined. Didn't she know that from now on, the hole would always be there?

Catherine wept a little, dabbing her eyes with a Kleenex. Much later, I believed that she was feeling the pain for all three of us. My mother was focusing on my suffering, wondering how I could be so brave. She didn't know I wasn't feeling anything.

For the moment, I was a spectator. The numbness moved me in and out of indifference. I talked about how I would have an angel in heaven, and reminisced about how God had been preparing me for this in the hospital.

Was it only Catherine who had entered the darkness, and who had begun to grieve for Jeremy?

When they arrived home, Janet and Johnny were devastated. I sat up, alert, as Charles dropped down on the couch next to me. He began to cry.

"It's my fault, it's my side of the family." Charles has a slight heart condition and was willing to take the blame. Instantly, I was holding him, telling him firmly that it was a chance thing, as the doctors had said, and nothing genetic. He calmed himself and told me about their visit.

"When we got there a nurse was holding him, rocking him in a rocking chair." I began to tremble all over. "I held him and rocked him, too." Janet had held him, and Johnny, dear Johnny. My world came crashing in around me, as the image of my husband holding his dying son forced its way into my consciousness.

"Was he awake?" I whispered, struggling to hold myself together.

"Off and on. His eyes would open and then he would go back to sleep. I think they've got him sedated."

Each question and each answer was like a dagger in my heart. "Is he eating?"

"Yes, a little." Still trying, little Jeremy. It's no use.

Everyone was crying. He's still alive, he's real, I thought. He's not gone yet. He opens his eyes, he eats a little.

Pain engulfed me. After a while, the incessant tears flooded in to wash away the images that were causing them.

Night had descended into the room, but no one bothered to turn on a light. We sat together in the darkness and the silence. There was nothing more we could do; we knew that now, convinced, finally, by Janet and Johnny and Charles, who were witnesses. And yet, a small hope seized me: Was there still one more way that I could care for my son?

"Charles," I noticed that my voice seemed to startle everyone. "He hasn't been baptized. We must call a priest, maybe one of our friends. . . ?"

My husband's hand on mine stopped me.

"I called for the hospital chaplain," he said gently, "and he baptized him." Charles paused, and I looked into those beautiful brown eyes, dulled now with sadness and pain. "I'm sorry, Mol, I don't remember his name."

And so I resigned myself to the finality. Whoever this priest was, I hoped, he must have known that my baby's name was Jeremy.

Eventually it was time for bed. I took my pills. Charles and I held each other again, talking. And as we talked, I knew I was in danger. And then I was sobbing and I heard my own voice crying out, "I want my baby!"

*I want my baby.* The words possessed me, crashing again and again against the fragile walls of my faltering spirit. Oh God, I thought, I can't stop it anymore. I'm breaking apart.

Charles held me for a long, long time. Eventually, the voice dimmed, and the walls stopped crumbling. I succumbed to the numbing effect of the drugs, and to the more ancient opiate of exhaustion.

On Friday morning, Charles went to work for a while. I didn't want him to go, but I knew it would give him something to do. He promised that he would take me for a ride in the afternoon. I looked forward to moving away from the couch, the rectangular windowpanes, the falling leaves.

We drove across town to see Robert, who owned a bakery. Charles left me in the car and went into the building. Soon they emerged together, walking slowly toward me, Charles talking, Robert listening. When they got to the car, Robert hugged me. He said he couldn't believe it. I said that I felt bad because the baby was born on his birthday. It would have been so nice.

Later that evening, Robert brought Donna to see me. In the haze of those days, a few things stood out. Donna's visit was one of them. Apparently she had insisted on the visit immediately, terribly upset but determined to do what she had to do. She rushed through the front door and was in tears before she sat down next to me on the couch. We cried together.

"This is so terrible," she said over and over. I observed that she wasn't at a loss for words like most everyone else. After a while she put her hands on my shoulders and looked me squarely in the eyes.

"Molly, we're going to do this together. You're not going to be alone; I can't believe this has happened, but it has, and we're going to make it, together."

I remembered that Donna's father had died only a few months earlier. Had someone said those words to her? They were so comforting. She was so sure. We would do whatever we had to do together.

Each day Dr. Geraty called and said the same thing. The baby was getting weaker, but was not uncomfortable. He didn't think that it would be too long. I hoped not. Once more he assured me that I shouldn't come down to the hospital. There was nothing I could do. I wanted to believe him. Inside, I felt a vague sense of relief, but I wished that he wouldn't talk about it. What would everyone think if they knew?

On Saturday I took my pills and waited. Charles' grandmother came by. I was surprised to learn that she had gone to see her great-grandson. I worried about who else had gone. Maybe they weren't telling me.

"He's just beautiful. It's too bad." She tried and failed to hold back the tears. She and I exchanged a glance. How many times had I listened to the stories of her own young motherhood, a story now two, almost three generations past? And now, in that glance, her eyes were filled with the wisdom of a long, full, brave lifetime. She knows, I thought to myself. She knows so much more than I do.

That night our house was filled with relatives and friends. Nancy and Gerry came by, leaving Gregory with her mother. Nancy told me that her father cried when he broke the news to them. She said that all she could do was run to hold Gregory close to her. She must love her son so much, I thought.

Later we talked about Jeremy as an angel in heaven. Jeremy would be our link to forever. Nancy laughed typically and said, "Yes, he'll be little JeremyMia." There was a moment of awkward silence and a look of disapproval on my mother's face. But I loved my friend greatly then, as I do today. A nickname. Jeremy had a nickname. She had found me a flower in a vacant lot.

Rick and Terry, the couple we had asked to be the baby's godparents, joined the gathering. Soon everyone was laughing and things seemed quite normal. In the middle of a conversation, I decided I was tired and went to bed. Was I acting strangely, I wondered, when I abruptly said good-night and left the room? It didn't matter.

🙘 🙘

*Daybreak. My eyes follow the Angel of Death. . . .*
*My lips begin to whisper on their own: I don't understand,*
*I don't understand, no I shall never understand.*

—Elie Wiesel, *The Oath*

*Sunday.* Had it only been a week? Catherine came over early; my mother had stayed through most of the long days, quietly making sure our house was in order. At about 8:30 the phone rang. As I picked it up, I knew that Jeremy was no longer real. Oh no, I thought, I can wait longer, let him be real a little longer.

"Mrs. Fumia, this is Dr. Geraty. " His voice seemed to catch. I could hardly hear him. "The baby died about a half hour ago."

His name is Jeremy, I thought.

"There was no discomfort, no pain."

My mind moved slowly. He lived exactly a week. That's quite a long time, long enough to be a real person. But it's over now. He was, and now he isn't anymore. He isn't opening and closing his eyes. He isn't trying to eat or moving his long fingers. He isn't squirming or crying. His little heart isn't trying to be right anymore. All the things I knew about Jeremy had ceased to be.

"Have you thought about arrangements yet, Mrs. Fumia?"

"A little." I hesitated. "What do parents usually do?"

He still spoke softly, but his tone was more businesslike. "Well, we would like your permission for an autopsy. We will do that today, and then release the baby by early afternoon."

He remembered Charles' name. Hadn't anyone told him Jeremy's name?

He continued. "Parents do different things. Some go for the whole funeral, open casket, the whole bit." Of course we wouldn't do that. Had he lived long enough, was he real enough, for a funeral? "Others choose cremation. There are a lot of things in between, I suppose."

I had been thinking about cremation. It seemed appropriate.

He said that he would like to discuss "our case" in a few weeks, when things died down, and that he was very sorry. We hung up, and I moved reluctantly toward the door of our bedroom, stopping when I saw myself in the mirror above my dresser.

"Oh God," I murmured weakly, staring at my own face and wondering what I would do next. But the reflection just stared back, defeated, until I didn't want to look anymore.

My eyes dropped down to the dresser. The little medal with the blue ribbon I had been given in the hospital was resting on top of my jewelry box. I tried not to lose control. What happened to my baby? He must have been here once, I told myself, grasping the medal. This wasn't here when I left to go to the hospital. Surely this is a sign that something is different. I stood there for a few moments, waiting for the confusion to recede and my body to stop trembling. *This is all that is left, and I will keep it always.* I tucked the medal away in the bottom of the jewelry box and went into the living room, where Charles, Johnny and Catherine, and my own mother and father were waiting.

"He's gone," I choked, the tears beginning to flow again, unrestrained.

Charles was there quickly. "We knew it would happen," he said gently. "We know it's better this way."

And like so many others, that became our common belief, the ground upon which we might move ahead. We started to discuss the arrangements. Charles and I wanted to have a memorial Mass that night at the university chapel.

Catherine, who had been silent, began to think aloud. "That's pretty fast. How will we tell everyone?" She paused. "And besides, the baby won't be ready."

I reacted violently. "The baby won't be ready! What are you thinking of?"

*No one can look at my baby anymore. I can't look.*

Calm, I mentioned that we had been thinking about cremation.

"You just can't cremate that beautiful little boy," she cried, disbelieving. Her words annoyed me, but I decided that she must not understand. I understood. His spirit was all that mattered, and that was with God.

"What do you want, Catherine?" I asked wearily, struggling to focus.

"It's not what I want," she was suddenly gentle, "it's what

you want, of course. It's just that I thought we'd have a little service, something simple, something so that everyone can come. And they don't all have to go to the burial."

I couldn't keep up with her. What I want, I thought miserably, is for this to be over.

They continued to talk, but I knew I would no longer be safe if I stayed there with them. So I retreated further behind the wall of haze that was there now, whenever I needed it, protecting me from losing myself, from exploding with desire.

The waves of feeling subsided. Catherine doesn't understand. The ashes can end our waiting.

Charles' voice called me back. How would it be if he phoned a friend of his who was working for his father, a well-known mortician, to talk about our alternatives? He made the call in the other room, and was back in a few minutes. While he was gone no one said a word.

He sat beside me and took my hand. "Joe says he'll arrange to get him from the hospital and they'll use a little pine box— no embalming or anything like that. We can bury him in a plot in the children's cemetery."

Grateful tears flowed down Catherine's cheeks, and I sensed that we were all satisfied. There would be no service at the cemetery, only the memorial Mass that night. Later, in a few weeks, Charles suggested, maybe then we could go to the cemetery. I didn't think it mattered if we ever went.

On the way to the Mass, I thought dreamily about death. Dying is different, I decided, than anything I had ever imagined. Gone was the dark cloud of unknowing, and the familiar bursts of panic and fear. Instead, we were somehow inside of death, Jeremy and I, where beginnings and endings weren't so scary. Would continuing, too, be possible from here?

But as quickly as I sensed our connection, so pure and true,

I knew we were separating. My son, who had been behind me, just beginning the journey, rushed by quickly, hardly stopping at all, and now he was way ahead and disappearing into some new place, a good place, filled with wisdom.

*Dear God, let it be this child who will lead me through life's secrets, and give meaning to everything that is meaningless.*

With each painful step across the Mission Church gardens and down the hallway to the chapel, I came back to the present. Our friends and family had spent a busy afternoon. The chapel was packed with people. Friends, relatives, and even a few people I didn't know looked at me as I shuffled in on Charles' arm, but I felt a bubble go up around me, keeping us safely apart. Many people were crying, and I wondered what they were feeling. I couldn't comprehend the intensity of the emotions that were making the room swell and sway back and forth. I believed, through the now familiar fog that prevailed, that something good was happening.

The "Mass of the Angels" was celebrated. I waited for the priest, an old friend, to say Jeremy's name. He did, once, or so I thought, but then he seemed to forget. He called him "the child" or "this little one."

As the end approached, I leaned over to Charles and whispered, "Don't you think we should say something, you know, thank all these people for coming?"

Charles stood up and began to talk softly to the gathering. I watched him, wondering how deeply he was hurting. Most of the attention had been on me. Had he had time to grieve? My eyes moved to Charles' father, sitting on the other side of him. Love and grief. Johnny had started to cry, a gentle, loving father watching his firstborn son thanking people for coming to celebrate the life and death of another firstborn son. I was momentarily hypnotized by his struggle and by the profound love I was witnessing, knowing it was special, and something to be cherished and remembered by all of us, sons, daughters, and grandchildren of this wonderful man.

Charles stopped and I stood up and took his arm. "Yes, thank you everyone, from the bottom of our hearts." I didn't know what else to say. After a moment I added, "Please don't worry about us, we'll be all right."

The Mass ended and nearly everyone came over to talk to us. I smiled at each of them, receiving their embraces, wondering if I had been presumptuous. Maybe they weren't worrying about us. Maybe they were thinking about Jeremy. I wished that I had said something else.

Many people came by the house afterward. There was drinking and eating and laughing, until finally everyone thought to leave us alone. I wasn't sure that I wanted them to go; again, I was afraid of the silence of the night in our bed. I took my pills.

We held each other, as we had every night since the nightmare began. I stared into the darkness. What would I do tomorrow? Thoughts of my baby once warm in my arms, opening and closing his eyes, now lying cold and still somewhere in the night began to creep in. There were a few tears, one here, one there. I worked hard not to think or to question. Most of all, I didn't ask if anyone was holding him when he died.

I knew that if I held off the feelings long enough, sleep would take over. It did.

The next morning Jeremy John Fumia was buried under number 62 in the children's cemetery. No one was there.

# Breaks in
# the Silence

*Happy are those who close their eyes:
for them nothing changes.*

—Elie Wiesel, *The Town Beyond the Wall*

I am not sure when I first knew how wrong everything had been.

I believe there were moments of recognition—
breaks in the silence. But for the most part, almost six years
came and went without questions, much less answers. And all
the while, the wounds remained open, unattended, unhealed.

And I recall times when my spirit, longing for understanding, nudged me toward consciousness. I remember especially

the day after he died. My mother had arrived early in the morning to help with the house, and just to be there for me, a ritual that would be repeated many times during the weeks that it took me to recuperate. We were standing together in the bathroom, in front of the mirror. Was that really me staring back, looking so tired and pale? The image turned fuzzy.

Silently I reached for the bottle of pills that had been prescribed for me. My mother read the label over my shoulder: Valium. We watched together as I poured them down the toilet. I became determined to heal physically and to start my life again.

Later that day, Dr. Kara's office called. Had I ever had the German measles? My mother was sure that I hadn't. The nurse said that I should have an injection, right away if possible, so that I would not have to worry about the dangers of German measles during my next pregnancy.

My next pregnancy. Yes, that was all in the world I wanted. We could give the new baby Jeremy's room, because I hadn't brought him home. I was so thankful. It could have been so much worse.

My mother drove me to the office. "Of course you understand," the nurse said as she prepared the injection, "that you cannot become pregnant again for at least three months. This injection is the same as giving you a case of the German measles, and it is in the first three months of pregnancy that this disease almost always produces a deformed child."

I didn't want to wait three months. I added up all those months of waiting that had already passed and were still to come. What would I do all that time? The nurse walked toward me, smiling. I wanted to tell her we'd take our chances with the German measles.

"All finished," she said cheerfully.

Too late, I thought, fighting off a sense of panic. The nurse didn't say anything about my baby who had died the day before. Before I left the office, she handed me a prescription for three months' worth of birth control pills.

Six weeks later I went to see Dr. Kara for the regular post-partum check. I was anxious to see him and willing to talk. And I did talk, and I cried a little. He wrote on my chart, listening intently. Then he turned to me, smiling an empty smile, his hand on the doorknob.

"You'll have lots of babies." The door closed behind him.

The next day Dr. Kara's partner, Vincent Mancini, called to tell me that he would like to be my doctor. I wondered if Dr. Kara didn't want me anymore. And again I thought of his own dead ten-year-old son, and I knew that he must resent my grief over a week-old infant. Gratefully, I accepted Dr. Mancini's offer.

Exactly seven months after Jeremy's death, we discovered that a second baby was on the way. Everyone rejoiced at the news, and I hoped that soon everything would be made right again. Dr. Geraty had assured us that the odds were in our favor, and that there was every reason to believe that our future offspring would be normal.

I worried anyway. But not as much, apparently, as everyone expected me to. I tried not to think about Jeremy and the months of lost time—yet I knew somehow that I wasn't starting over. I was simply doing it all again. Even though Jeremy was not there, I settled for things being as there were. No, my struggle was not to be with my fears, but with my friends.

During those months of waiting, it seemed like every woman I knew had a baby. Baptisms and baby showers dotted our calendar. Jeremy's godparents asked us to be the godparents of their new son. Now and then I was jealous of the happiness of our friends, and I resented how easily they produced healthy children.

And sometimes, as I watched the new mother delighting in her infant, I would warn her silently: *Don't think you are ahead of me. I was a mother before you.*

I stubbornly insisted on fitting in with the other new mothers. In the fall of 1973, when I was six months pregnant, we joined a large group of friends for a picnic at a nearby park. Nancy and Gerry were there with one-year-old Gregory. Terry and Rick brought our godson, Jason. Our old friends Robert and Donna were happily spreading the news that their first child was due in February.

Some of the women sat in a group, chatting about pregnancy and delivery while a few toddlers played at their feet and new babies slept in their arms. It was a familiar scene: young mothers comparing notes on the harrowing experience of bringing a child into the world.

"When those pains really started to come," Nancy laughed, "I forgot everything they'd taught me. The problem then is just to survive."

I smiled at my friend. She is so wonderfully honest, I thought. Another friend of ours, Maryanne, who was expecting her first child any day, revealed some of the familiar fears even while she was trying to sound confident.

"I'm glad David will be there with me." She glanced over at her husband, who was cooking hamburgers with Charles and Robert. "We've practiced a lot. I'm sure he'll remind me of what I'm supposed to do."

Nancy looked at me and rolled her eyes. "I hope David doesn't get stuck in traffic," she remarked. Even Maryanne laughed.

At that point I spoke up about our delivery, the way my

labor had begun, how I had felt, how Charles had helped. David wandered over to our group while I was talking. When I had finished, he addressed me sternly.

"Molly," he began, putting his arm around Maryanne as if to protect her from me, "can't you see how scared she is? It would be better if you didn't say those things to her."

I stared at him. What things? That I went into labor? That Charles was there? That we delivered our child?

Anger and embarrassment engulfed me. I turned and walked away as fast as I could, in no particular direction, stopping only when I reached the grass by the lake.

No one understands. They can't change what has happened. I am a mother and no one can take that away.

Charles caught up with me and I threw myself into his arms. After a moment, he held me back from him, searching my face, his own etched in concern. Tearfully, I related the conversation.

"He's afraid, Mol," he told me solemnly. "He probably didn't mean anything. He just doesn't want Maryanne to worry."

"Charles," I protested, "anything can happen, you know. Once you're pregnant, you're vulnerable. Things don't fit together perfectly anymore. They'd better wake up."

We went home without saying good-bye to anyone. I waited all evening for David to call and apologize. But instead, they went to the hospital to have a beautiful, healthy baby girl.

❧ ❧

*I should have liked to know this little brother, both younger and older than myself. Whom did he resemble? My mother?*

—Elie Wiesel, *The Oath*

Vince Mancini delivered our second child, Melissa Ann, on January 3, 1974. 1 had a cold. I did not wear a mask while I nursed her, and she did not get my cold.

For the next three days, my hospital room was a madhouse. A constant flow of family and friends came to congratulate us and see our healthy daughter. Charles took armloads of flower arrangements and gifts home after each of his visits. Telegrams arrived from various parts of the country, and the phone never stopped ringing. Finally, a thoughtful nurse took my phone off the hook and closed the door when she found my room momentarily empty.

"I think you're breaking the record for baby celebration, " she remarked as she cleared away two empty champagne bottles from the night before. "Where did these come from?" she laughed.

I tried to explain. "You see, our first baby died. And everyone is very excited about Missy being healthy. They want to share the joy with us. This is the payoff, I suppose, for sharing the pain."

Even though I could explain it to the nurse, I was inwardly amazed by the jubilation that was going on around me. Two months after Missy came home, we baptized her in the same chapel where we had celebrated Jeremy's short life. Afterward, the christening party was held at Johnny's and Catherine's house.

With Missy in my arms, I moved from room to room, trying to talk to each of more than a hundred guests. Planning this party had been like planning another wedding. Besides all of our friends and the entire family on both sides, Catherine invited many of their old friends, all of whom had been there the night we had Jeremy's Mass. Then there were new friends, neighbors who had shared our misfortune, and others who had touched our lives and were somehow connected to the wonderful conclusion of these fourteen months of waiting.

It took two hours to open the gifts, but no one seemed to mind. We ate and drank and sang and danced long after Missy was safely tucked away in a crib in Charles' old bedroom.

Later, when everyone except our closest friends and family had gone, Johnny brought out an old and treasured bottle of wine and handed it to his son.

"Open it, Charles," he commanded, "and we will drink one more toast together to Melissa Ann Fumia."

We all raised our glasses and cheered the sleeping infant, and the room and that night were enveloped in love and in hope for the future.

The future developed quickly. Mark Joseph was born on July 26, 1975. Like his sister, he was delivered without anesthesia, and nursed until he was eight months old.

Everyone was glad to have another baby boy, a healthy little heir. From what I could remember, Mark didn't look at all like Jeremy; he had fair skin and blond hair. Having a girl and a boy was nice, I told myself. If I still had Jeremy, one of these children may not have come along. I felt more complete than I had in a long time. And when we again celebrated the birth of our healthy son with a rousing christening party, I felt a happiness that was indescribable.

ᴋ᷿ ᴋ᷿

*The question remains open and no new fact can change it.*

—Elie Wiesel, *A Beggar in Jerusalem*

I developed a way of dealing with Jeremy's memory. I understood only vaguely that I had some needs where he was concerned, and I struggled to fulfill them without ever asking where they came from or what they meant. When I was pregnant with Mark, I would always explain to anyone who asked that this would be my third child. Invariably, they would pursue the conversation, wanting to know if I had one of each sex, their ages, their names, and I would then have to add, "We lost our first little boy."

This conversation reoccurred often. My questioner would always be made to feel sad and embarrassed, which sometimes satisfied me, sometimes distressed me. And to say that we had "lost" a child was never quite right. Did we lose him, or did he die, or both?

One thing was clear. I was obsessed with his name. Jeremy John. I loved to say it. It was my way of identifying his reality. He really existed; I have another son, I would insist to myself.

His name seemed so important. Catherine understood about names. When she had her first son, she insisted that he be named Charles John, in order to remember Johnny's brother. Then, fifteen years later, they named their second son John Charles. Many of their friends teased them, sure that they had somehow gotten stuck. But it wasn't that at all. She understood that each of those names must be remembered, celebrated, and carried on. They must never be lost or forgotten.

In May 1976, when Mark was ten months old, I discovered that a fourth child would arrive the following February. Since Jeremy, each pregnancy had been proclaimed a great blessing. But this time my enthusiasm was tempered a bit by the thought of three babies only three years apart.

To make matters worse, no one seemed to view pregnancy

the way I did. They said things that confused me and made me angry.

For instance, one day a friend of mine casually asked why I would want another child when I already had a boy and a girl.

"I suppose we have to break the tie," I snapped.

She laughed uneasily, but I continued to glare at her, thinking about how much she had to learn, and about how for us the tie was already broken.

What is happening to me, I asked myself as that moment passed. What else is there? But the answers were still years away.

In August I miscarried at about fourteen weeks. The experience was horrible. Two weeks of bleeding, wondering, not knowing what to pray for. I finally "spontaneously aborted" the baby late on a Friday afternoon in Dr. Mancini's office. The next week, when I went back in to see him, we talked about the miscarriage. I don't recall how the conversation started, only how it ended. I had become enraged.

"Do you remember?" I demanded, aware of the fact that my voice was rising and the door to his office was wide open. I slammed my hand down on the examination table.

"I was lying right here, blood all over me. Your nurse was annoyed that I had made such a mess. So I apologized. I actually apologized!"

"You shouldn't have done that, Molly. It wasn't your fault. "

"She didn't seem to think so, Vince. She accepted my apology." I stared at him, but he didn't say anything. He wasn't willing, I suppose, to challenge my version of the events.

"Do you remember now? Here I was, tears streaming down my face, mourning for my baby that you insisted on calling an embryo." I paused for a moment, watching him, not caring how much what I was saying might hurt him.

"But you didn't notice," I continued, allowing my anger to choose the words, "because my blood and what was left of my child had clogged up your sink."

Color drained from his face. He was crushed. I was surprised. I went home wondering if there were other things I needed to feel and say. For the moment, I had said enough.

I decided to take a break from having children. I had expended so much energy in having them, and in losing them, that big pieces of my life had been neglected or forgotten.

Missy and Mark delighted me, yet I felt restless and incomplete. In the spring of 1976 I went on a retreat to attempt to weave the various strands of my life, which seemed to be waving aimlessly about, back together.

Gradually, I rediscovered my spiritual self, and I came to appreciate the small moments I found for quiet in the middle of my noisy days. It was for me an exciting time of spiritual exploration. I began seeing things differently, connecting what I could glimpse of the spiritual universe with the rather terrifying signs of our times. I felt more whole, more alive than I had in a long while.

Inevitably, that newly empowered spirit rekindled my longstanding social and political concerns. Taking the children along with me, I plunged into social activism. I became more involved with the poor in our area, and we all helped out at a local soup kitchen and shelter for the homeless. I studied the connections between poverty and militarism, and attended gatherings that deplored both. I joined other Catholics who were striving to integrate spirituality and work for justice and peace in their lives, and found in those communities some extraordinary individuals and lifelong friends.

Charles was not about to become a social activist. But our conversations were again sprinkled with questions of politics and economics as well as Missy's progress at nursery school or Mark's tangles with the little boy next door. He tried hard to be supportive and helpful as I juggled the various parts of my life to fit into days that were only twenty-four hours long. Somehow, the children kept up with me and I with them. Our lives together were turning out differently than either Charles or I had imagined, yet it seemed that we were beckoned forward and promised a way to make it all work.

Life became fuller and faster. There was no time for remembering.

> The living person I was, the one I thought myself
> to be, had been living a lie; I was nothing more than an
> echo of voices long since extinguished. . . . I thought I
> was living my own life, but I was only inventing it.

—Elie Wiesel, A Beggar in Jerusalem

It happened about a year after my confrontation with Vince Mancini. I was at a church with a group of people I didn't know very well. We were talking, sharing with each other the single experience in our lives that had most affected what we each experienced as faith. I talked about Jeremy, about how he had helped me feel close to God and unafraid of death. I talked about knowing him only for a week, and what a gift that had been. Everyone was moved, and impressed with my ability to transcend the loss of a child and emerge spiritually renewed. One person, a young man, reflected the thoughts of the group.

"Really living life to the fullest sometimes means being with those we love in death. In that short time, your son had a wonderful mother."

The smile that I had been directing toward him froze on my face. Over and over again, shocking words of accusation penetrated my being: *It didn't happen that way. That's not what happened. You lied.*

I drove home trembling. To my horror, the days of that week now six years past came into focus. The hazy dream became a nightmare. I pushed it away. It pursued me. *You never knew him. You didn't see him after Tuesday. You didn't hold him after Monday.* I walked into the house where my two small children were playing. He was a person, a human being just like them. Who would he have been? *You never knew him. You could have known more; there were five more days between the last time you saw him and the day he died. It's different than the way you tell it. You weren't a good mother in the short time you had. They only think you were. You lied.*

I picked up little Mark and held him close to me. Gradually my heart stopped pounding and the feelings faded away. By the next day, life appeared to have slipped back into the ordinary.

But something had changed. There was to be no further retreat into oblivion. The numbness had been pierced.

*God of my childhood, show me the way to my self.*

—Elie Wiesel, *The Town Beyond the Wall*

After a break of three and a half years, I gave birth to Nicholas John on December 7, 1978. The pregnancy had been rocky; I almost miscarried and was confined to the couch for many weeks. When he finally arrived, perfect and beautiful, a brown-haired, olive-skinned little boy, I decided that God and I were now even.

It would take still another pregnancy to bring me back to center stage with my firstborn son.

More than seven years had passed since Jeremy's death. It was the spring of 1980. From the very beginning of this new nine months of waiting, I was aware of a strong yet unspoken sense of alarm that I was carrying around with my unborn infant. I was much more worried about the health of this baby than I had ever been while I carried Missy, Mark, or even Nicholas, whom I had almost lost. Why, I asked myself, after three healthy children, am I convinced that this child would not be all right?

And there was something else going on. As the baby I carried came to life, every kick signaled a warning: The memories were there, gathered at the edge of my consciousness, waiting to be called forth to testify.

On several occasions, the silence was broken. We would begin to talk, Charles and I, or once with Johnny and Catherine, and another time with some old friends, about the past—about Jeremy. To me, the truth of what happened was becoming too apparent to ignore. So I would say the words: *"I wasn't there when he died."*

And I would think, the doctor said not to go. But I shouldn't have listened. If only I could tell the story again, differently.

Charles and the others always tried to comfort me.

"You were so young then," Johnny and Catherine excused my behavior.

"You did the best you could," Charles reminded me gently. "You can't blame yourself for what happened."

Certainly they loved me, but they didn't understand. I didn't blame myself for what happened. He died. No one could have stopped his dying. But what about what didn't happen? Someone must take the blame for the loneliness of a dying child. There were times when I thought I would explode. The months wore on, and the anxieties grew and multiplied, stealing my energy, making me less and less present to my children, my husband and my daily life.

But somehow, as always, that life went on. Summer came upon us. Missy and Mark learned to swim and Nicholas learned to run. Like mothers everywhere, I followed my youngest around, rescuing Nicholas from disaster, and rescuing our household treasures from Nicholas.

In late August, when I was about eight months pregnant, I went to New York to attend a conference at the United Nations. One of the other participants was a nurse who specialized in nursing psychology. Amid stimulating talk of Third World development and the economics of justice, Pat and I found each other.

We connected immediately. She was also struggling to remain involved in global concerns while changing diapers and driving carpools. She drew me into conversation as soon as we met, congratulating me for my presence at the conference despite such an advanced state of pregnancy. I found myself revealing a little of my story; I had four children already, but one had died. We discussed his medical problem and she asked questions about my other pregnancies. I was nervous. She was getting close.

During the next free afternoon, we talked again about my son. Thoughts I had left unspoken for years began to pour forth. The baby I was carrying kicked and poked, encouraging me, urging me to consider something new. An hour passed.

Two hours. Finally, I knew I could no longer bury the feelings that were burning a hole in my heart. The long-held secret must be told. It had been long enough.

Trembling, I began my confession.

"He needed me and I wasn't there."

Pat started to interrupt.

"No, let me say this," I pleaded with her, remembering all of the others who had ever tried to "comfort" me. "Please let me say this. The one person Jeremy needed was the only person he had known for nine months, and I wasn't there. Other people could try, but he needed his mother to love him and help him die."

My shame was choking me. I had never felt so close to despair.

"He was alone, all alone. While he was dying, I was watching the leaves, and thinking about my pain. I should have held him and kissed him. I should have been there to love him. He needed me."

Pat was holding me, urging me gently to go on.

"I just want him to forgive me."

I let myself sink into long, uncontrolled sobs and Pat waited, her arms still around me.

"Molly," she began carefully, "we know now that neonatal death is a very traumatic experience for parents, especially for the mother. Doctors are changing their approach, urging parents to be with their babies, even if they are dying. This is very difficult, because those feelings of confusion and pain are powerful. We're just trying to help them through it."

For an instant, I wondered what it would have been like to have known Pat seven years before. But the thought brought back my most private fears. . . . Surely I would have run from her. I couldn't have survived the knowing.

"I believe," she continued, "what happened to you is that doctors, well-meaning people, and the miracle of drugs kept you from the process of grief. I doubt that you've done it yet. You were never allowed to say good-bye. You never went through the psychological stages of disbelief, denial, anger, and acceptance. You never started to mourn because you were kept from the object of your mourning."

She stopped to watch me. I was totally immersed in her words.

"If I were you, Molly, I would be terribly, terribly angry. But besides that, you must take this day, this very moment, to begin your period of mourning."

I was afraid to believe her. I didn't want to blame anyone. I had never blamed the doctors, my family, or even God for what I suspected was my enormous violation of motherhood. I had believed that I should take responsibility for the things I did and didn't do.

Pat's eyes locked into mine. "And Molly, don't be afraid to remember the way it was. You were different then, younger, not nearly as experienced or as wise as you are now. That's not an excuse, Molly. That's a fact."

I looked down at my bulging abdomen, caressing it gently. Something seemed to be changing. For so long, I had only pretended to understand. Perhaps there really was an explanation for my behavior that wasn't make-believe.

"I have always needed to acknowledge Jeremy's existence, to claim him as my son," I said, nodding to myself as I spoke. "Maybe that was because I never got to be his mother. I didn't know how it felt to be a mother. Now I do."

I hesitated, but Pat was also nodding her head firmly. With some small surge of confidence, I went on.

"If it happened now, I don't think that I would be so afraid.

Perhaps I could somehow find the courage to help my child die. If I could do it all again, I would hold him. He would know how loved he was, even if he was dying."

Pat reacted quickly.

"Jeremy knew you loved him, Molly, but some of the people around you didn't know that. In their desire to shield you from pain, they lost you to it."

We walked around tree-lined New York streets for another hour, talking about the things I could do to continue the process of grief that had begun. A gravestone and funeral might help. I would try not to blame myself. I would consider who it was that needed to be forgiven.

I came home from New York knowing that the remembering had been good for me. What I didn't know was that it was necessary for my very survival. For while I was confronting my past, in no way was I owning it. A chance telephone conversation with my mother began to illuminate this need.

I rarely shared my most intimate thoughts with her, but on this day I needed to talk, and I was grateful she was there. I told her about Pat and my experience in New York. As I talked, I began to sense that this conversation might lead to disaster, but I was compelled to go on. I talked about the doctors and the drugs. I confided in her that recently I had been trying to deal with some painful memories. I should never have told her that I wanted to buy a gravestone.

She was quick to respond.

"I wanted a gravestone at the time," she said, "but you said no, so I thought I shouldn't interfere." From that moment on, any trace of love in her voice was lost to me; where she poured forth her own anguish; all I was able to hear was self-pity. "You say you didn't grieve. Well, I know that I grieved. You don't know how I grieved. I was just so upset. That darling little boy."

She went on, recalling her own sleepless nights and lonely tears. With each word, my anger mounted.

Struggling to sound calm, I spoke deliberately. "I was just trying to share with you some of my feelings." Was she the child or was I?

There was what I thought to be a dramatic sigh on the other end of the line. "Molly, I just don't want to talk about this anymore. I just can't."

Inside of me, the anger exploded into rage. After a terse good-bye, I slammed down the receiver. The phone toppled off the counter, and I kicked it across the room. Just then Charles walked in.

"How dare she!" I shouted for all the neighbors to hear. "How dare she take my pain and make it hers!" I was sure that she had stolen the only tie I had with my son.

"She can't have it. He was my baby, not hers. Can't she even allow me suffering of my very own?"

After a while my husband, who had been listening patiently, took my trembling hands into his. Without a trace of unbelief, he looked into my eyes.

"Your mother loves you, and she loved Jeremy. She, too, had needed to grieve."

I started to object.

"Molly, I do understand your feelings. But just who is it that you are so angry at?"

I didn't know. I didn't want to know. Eventually I understood that I would never confront my mother with those ugly feelings. The baby was due to arrive soon. I was afraid that I would become so angry that I would deny her the pleasure of her new grandchild. Anyway, it would take too much energy, energy I didn't have to give, to confront her, and to confront myself.

I wondered how my unborn child was surviving this emotional roller-coaster.

> The real problem isn't hate, no not hate.
> But shame, yes, shame.

—Elie Wiesel, The Gates of the Forest

One night, a week before delivery, I had a dream. I had delivered another baby boy. He was sick, just as Jeremy had been. Same condition, same story, same cast of characters . . . except for me. I acted entirely differently. In the dream I never let him go. I cried, I grieved, I felt devastation, but I never let him go. I told him that I loved him, and he died in my arms. Then I woke up.

Lying in bed, I replayed the dream, examining its meaning. I could hardly believe it. Could it be that the fear I had been feeling about the health of the new baby might actually be about a second chance? Was I daring God to give me another sick child, so that I could prove that I would act differently? It seemed so clear.

I am different, I thought. I am who I am now. Just to be sure, I pleaded with God to send me a healthy child. I didn't want any mix-ups.

Gino James was born on October 10, 1980, healthy and perfect. His name was a source of delight—we had decided on an Italian name, and Gino came out looking a like Sean Patrick. Nevertheless, Gino was christened at a huge party in true Italian style.

The Jeremy feelings, now so familiar, all but disappeared during the busy activity of Gino's first year. But after his birthday, with what would have been Jeremy's ninth birthday approaching, I began to remember again, and the pain came rushing back, this time with more vengeance than ever before. Panic. Humiliation, depression, desire that would never be fulfilled. In all the years before, it had never been like this. I couldn't talk about him; I couldn't even mention his name. I hid from the thoughts, terrified of the feelings that would always follow.

November 12, 1981. My vision of hell arrived disguised as Jeremy's birthday. I did not know who I was or who I had been. I lived and died in a single day.

*I feel the wound reopening. From the depth of the*
*abyss, the years soar up, unchecked, snatching my heart and*
*pounding it violently against my chest. Anguish grips me,*
*as though I were about to meet something as absolute,*
*as decisive, as pure as the death of a child at dawn.*

—Elie Wiesel, *A Beggar in Jerusalem*

In desperation, I reached out to a loving friend, one who had not heard my story before. I craved reassurance and affirmation.

Even over the phone her voice filled me with hope. I was searching for the magic words that would bring me peace. She was loving, as always, deeply moved by my obvious pain. In a moment of silence, I knew that the words I needed would not come from her. I had been foolish to expect them. The only magic was her great love for me.

"What I do sometimes, when I'm missing someone I've loved, is I talk to them in my prayer. It makes me feel close again."

It was a good idea, I thought, but I was afraid of what Jeremy might say.

During the rest of the day, the nightmare continued. Charles was there again, as he had been many times before. I sensed him struggling to get inside of my pain, trying to make a difference. I had long since stopped expecting him to share my suffering. His grief was his own. At least he had said good-bye.

I awoke on November 13 sick with exhaustion. Alone in our bed, I felt trapped in total futility. The children came in, climbing into bed with me, shouting their good-mornings, beginning their day. I looked at them through empty eyes, as if I wasn't sure they were real. Suddenly I was aware that I was missing precious moments. What were they saying? Did one of them need me? The nightmare of the day before was a thief, robbing me of that which mattered most. I knew that radical change was needed . . . for their sake, and for mine.

On November 14, I ordered a simple flat marker for Jeremy's grave.

On December 13, I went to see Carl Geraty. He was very open and warm, not at all the way I remembered him. I told my story. His head bowed, he listened quietly. I told him that I felt it might be more helpful to explain to parents their options, and urge them to be with their children. Had he changed his philosophy in recent years?

He looked up. "You're being very kind, Molly. I remember what happened. I kept you from your child, as did your other doctors, the drugs and even your extended family, however loving they thought they were being.

"I would never do that today. We urge parents to be close to their infants and to begin the grief process. We help them go through each step, to find some way to live with dying."

I felt satisfied and relieved. The responsibility really hadn't been all mine. I was thankful for his honesty. Before I left, he reached out and grasped my hands firmly.

"Molly, don't get me wrong. You're a vital, loving human being who is living with a very painful problem. We have to do something about that birthday before next year."

He gave me the name of a psychologist.

> His face grew hard: "You're my friend and I want to know everything."
>
> I trembled, my breathing quickened, my nostrils flared. He wants to know everything, I thought. He isn't afraid to know everything.
>
> —Elie Wiesel, *The Town Beyond the Wall*

One week after Christmas, I walked into the office of Dr. Terry Johnston. I had advised many friends to seek counseling, but when it came to taking my own advice, I felt anxious and self-conscious.

Those feelings evaporated quickly. Terry had ten children of her own. We shared similar political views, spiritual struggles, and what Terry called "our best guess about parenting." I was enjoying her immensely when she reminded me that it was time to tell my story.

The words poured out easily. While she listened, Terry's face seemed to swallow me up with compassion. When I was done, she smiled broadly.

"Guess what?"

I smiled back, curious.

"My birthday is November 12."

Despite the solemnity of the moment, we laughed together at such a coincidence. A sign. I couldn't hope for much more; I would trust her completely.

"There is something inside of you, Molly, that is keeping you from being whole. You must confront it and own it, so that you can be who you are."

She walked me to the door. She was so confident.

"You can do it. I'll help you. We'll do it together."

And so I began to remember. But this time, it would be different.

> *They walked, and the steps echoing more or less*
> *together off the sidewalk said: No, you are not alone,*
> *but two, two, two.*

—Elie Wiesel, *The Town Beyond the Wall*

Shortly after my dear friend suggested it, I tried to go to Jeremy in prayer. Afterward, I even wrote it down, hoping I might never forget. It brought me some amount of consolation, and yet. . . .

During my meditation a heavenly being (who I thought might be Jesus or perhaps an angel) came to take me to God. He had to tug at me because I was reluctant to go and seemed to be stuck in my place. But he kept trying, gathering me up more and more firmly in his arms. Finally I let go, and we went off.

We were floating, and I was very happy. I buried my head in his shoulder and closed my eyes, allowing myself to be a child again. He leaned down his head to cover me up even more. His arms seemed enormous and safe.

When I finally looked up, I saw a brilliant light, and I could feel love radiating from its center, and I knew it must be God. Then my infant son was brought to me, wrapped up securely in a soft blanket. He began to nuzzle at my breast, and then he nursed eagerly. Gradually he was content, and I watched him drift off to sleep in my arms.

It was as if time had not gone by. My child knew me and I knew him. He didn't seem to care about anything except being with me. Why was that, I asked myself? I thought it might be that he was to close to the Creator and to the beginning and end of everything. All he knew was to love wholly and unconditionally. I held him, taken by this moment, yet unaccountably anxious to move on.

The prayer was a gift. Yet even so great a gift was not enough.

# Entering
the Night

*Thank you, my boy. Thank you for disturbing me, shaking me. Thank you for crossing my path. I desperately needed you. Thank you for forcing my hand; you did it in time.*"

—Elie Wiesel, *The Oath*

For the moment, what had seemed like an endless emotional crisis passed. My time with Terry was a luxury that I deeply appreciated. I didn't know exactly where all of this was leading, but I was finally willing to proceed.

Order returned to my life. Indeed, order was a necessity; my days overflowed with the demands of raising four small children. Beyond the family, I had decided that my political and social concerns needed a stronger, even formalized spiritual base. Gradually, I emptied my calendar of meetings and activities so that I could spend my precious time away from the children in a single pursuit: I would seek a master's degree in theology at the Graduate Theological Union in Berkeley.

Charles had gone to graduate school earlier in our marriage, and was enthusiastic about my endeavor. But even with his help, the children's enormous needs and unpredictable daily lives limited me to taking just one class each quarter.

It didn't matter. In fact, I wanted to go slowly, so as to savor all the things I was learning. Each course I chose seemed to be better than the last. In the beginning, I was especially drawn to courses on Scripture, both the Old and New Testaments. But my favorite courses by far were those that mixed religion and politics.

In January 1982 I fought the long lines of registration to enroll in a class in liberation theology that would be taught by a well-known author and Protestant theologian, Robert McAfee Brown. The course engaged us in a new approach to religion and politics, as seen through the eyes of the oppressed. I was fascinated, and thoroughly enlightened. I was also deeply impressed with Bob Brown.

So as the new quarter began in April, and despite the fact that this was hardly the way to pursue my academic career, I decided to enroll in whatever course Bob would be teaching. "The Theology of Wiesel's Novels" was how it read on the class schedule. In the registration line, I found out that the course was about a close friend of Bob's, a Jewish writer. It didn't really matter. If Robert McAfee Brown chose him, so would I. And in that way, Elie Wiesel entered my life.

"In the beginning," Bob told us on the first day of class, "the message of Elie Wiesel will not be a comfortable discovery. "

It was true. It was a dreadful awakening.

I had returned home from that first day curious enough. After the children were in bed, I picked up our first assignment, the book *Night,* Elie Wiesel's account of the horrifying events of his past. Tired as I was, I couldn't stop reading.

What is it that happened when I met Elie Wiesel? *Try to remember everything.*

Bob had begun the story in class that day. Elie was only fourteen when he and his family were taken from their hometown of Sighet, in Transylvania, to the Nazi death camp at Auschwitz. On the night he arrived, his mother and little sister, Tzipora, were sent to the right, and Elie and his father went to the left. Elie remembers only an instant of this parting that would be forever. The "right," at Auschwitz, meant fire and death.

Then Bob shared with us excerpts from Elie's writings. I believed I had some understanding of the Holocaust. But the power of this survivor's words retold the story until I knew I understood nothing. The event is unspeakable, Elie Wiesel insists, and yet he dares to speak. . . . Image upon image, testimony upon testimony, the suggestion of suffering and death too terrible, too inconsolable for the memory of any but the dead themselves. Indeed, we must enter not only the tale, but also the telling.

Despite Bob's careful introduction, I was not prepared for the experience of reading the memories of this storyteller. The power of Elie's remembering invaded my imagination, pulling me deeper into the abyss of sin that destroyed a whole people, a past, present, and future, and even a God.

The pages of Elie's *Night* led me, as so many others had been led, into the darkest corner of human history, to recall and to witness the consummate evil that thrived there:

*Never shall I forget that night, the first night in camp, which has turned my life into one long night, seven times cursed and seven times sealed. Never shall I forget the smoke. Never shall I forget the little faces of the children, whose bodies I saw turned into wreaths of smoke beneath a silent blue sky.*

*Never shall I forget those flames which consumed my faith forever.*

*Never shall I forget that nocturnal silence which deprived me, for all eternity, of the desire to live.*

*Never shall I forget those moments which murdered my God and my soul and turned my dreams to dust.*

*Never shall I forget these things, even if I am condemned to live as long as God himself. Never.*

—Elie Wiesel, *Night*

Scarcely believing, I read these words over and over. Elie's version of reality threatened the limits of what I had thought to be possible. How could this be, I thought to myself, that little children were burned alive on a pile of wood and petrol? Why, why, why, in a world where children ask only to be lifted up into our arms and comforted? The answer, I found, was that the children were burned alive because the gas chambers were full of adults.

The logic of Auschwitz.

I returned to class the next week in a considerably more somber mood. My classmates, too, had been shaken by Wiesel's story. Bob helped us along, taking us back, again and again, through the tragic events.

I found myself mysteriously drawn to this man. I thought of him as Elie and used his first name when I spoke of him in class. I devoured the assignments, memorized phrases, yearned to get inside of his spellbinding words and perfect sentences. There was a lesson here for me, as yet unclear. And there was urgency— it was as if my own survival was dependent upon his.

No one, it seemed to me, could continue after the loss of everything and everyone he had ever known and loved. Indeed, for a long time it seemed to Elie that death had triumphed. For him, there were ten years of self-imposed silence. But eventually he broke that silence with *Night*, the devastating recollection of the precise events, just as they happened, which marked not only "the death of his childhood" and the murder of his family, but the extermination of six million Jews, a million and a half children. Elie Wiesel had come to understand that survival meant never to forget.

This was his secret: He survived by remembering. His memories stalked him, intent upon the kill, until he turned to face them. The ghosts tormented him, sure of his fear, until he told their story. The curse of remembering was harsh, but there was a blessing, too. This knowing, which finally made holy the evidence of the past, was a transforming grace.

✍ ✍

In the days that followed, I read on, searching especially for Elie's memories of the children. I cried; I died a little inside. Anytime he mentioned them, my heart would threaten to break. First, there were the little children being delivered into the pit of fire in *Night*. Then, in *Dawn* and *Ani Maamin*, there was the baby who wouldn't stop crying, and the mother whose smothering hand silenced him forever in a futile attempt to save the others. There was Tevye the Tailor's ten children, some who couldn't even stand on their own feet, who lined up from oldest to youngest in front of a firing squad, holding hands to die together in *A Beggar in Jerusalem*. And Mendele, in *The Town Beyond the Wall*, never shall I forget Mendele, who kept the vow of silence through a horribly painful death to try to save the woman who had given him life.

Then it began to happen. When Elie remembered a million and half children, I remembered my own. The hand of the little boy holding onto Madame Schacter became my Nicholas' hand, trembling as he grows ever more fearful of the fire that will take them, too; the "little faces of the children, whose bodies I saw burned into wreaths of smoke," became the faces of my Melissa and Mark; the baby who had to be silenced became my Gino, telling me in the only way he knows how that he is afraid.

These were frightening, anxious moments of connection. Elie's story was devastating, yet the temptation to remain there with him and the ghosts of the children was too strong to resist. And when I did let go, my soul was deeply disturbed with hideous imaginings. A child, *perhaps my child*, wrenched from my arms, thrown onto pyre, writhing and screaming. I could hear it, a tiny baby scream in the night. *There was a time and place where this had actually come to pass.*

The gruesome death of a helpless, innocent child . . . the image was almost too much to bear. But still I turned the pages of Elie's memories, and I came to a mother who watched her firstborn disappear into the night. Not a single touch, no lasting embrace, no good-bye. And I knew.

I had entered, in the small way that I could, into Elie's experience. His recollections were so vivid, so deeply meaningful, and now strangely familiar. We had all fallen under his spell, seduced by the sacred truths that emerged from his memory of total, unspeakable suffering. But for me, there was something else.

> *What is at stake is your life, your survival!*
> *Do not forget, do not forget!*
>
> —Elie Wiesel, *Souls on Fire*

In May 1982 I learned I was to come face to face with the man whose message had so captivated me. Bob had arranged for members of the class to meet with his friend after his lecture at the university in the more intimate setting of the Jewish Center Library. I approached this event sure that destiny had somehow arranged things correctly. Of course I must meet him. I must know more.

Charles and I arrived early for the lecture and found seats with the rest of my class. Bob gave me a warm smile when we came in. Does he sense, I wondered, how much this man has come to mean to me? We waited while the large auditorium filled with people, many of them wearing yarmulkes. Again, I felt strangely close to the storyteller; these were his people, the generation after the six million, and the next generation after them. Elie walked onto the stage and sat down at a little desk, looking quite like the rebbe, I decided.

His talk was wonderful, although I was distracted by his voice. It was gentle, yet firm and unafraid; it was sad and mysterious, yet delightful to listen to. Afterward we walked to a nearby Jewish center for our private time with him.

The "private" meeting turned out to be about fifty lucky guests crowded into a room already bursting with books. Obviously, we had entered a little corner of Elie's world. We wandered around the shelves, stopping to look at a copy of the *Torah,* and I tried to imagine Elie's childhood as a student in Sighet.

The chairs and couches filled quickly, and the guests, who included my classmates, Jewish students from the center, and a few others who had simply heard a rumor about Elie's visit, waited with obvious excitement for the start of the discussion. Bob had asked us to prepare questions for Elie beforehand; he wanted no awkward silences or slow beginnings. I watched the two of them sitting together on a well-worn couch, their heads bent in quiet conversation. How nice it would be to be sitting with them, I imagined, not to intrude, but for a small taste of their sweet friendship.

As I waited for a chance to ask a question, I wondered how in the world Bob could have ever doubted us. It seemed quite clear that everyone in the room had something to ask Elie Wiesel.

He listened to each question intently, and answered each one of us in a voice that was so quiet, there was hardly another sound in the room as we strained to hear every word. He seemed very weary and as always, very sad.

> *I hear a voice within me telling me to stop*
> *mourning the past. I too want to sing of love and of its*
> *magic. I too want to celebrate the sun, and the dawn*
> *that heralds the sun.*
>
> —Elie Wiesel, "Why I Write"

After about an hour Bob closed off the discussion. The guests stood around and shared coffee and more informal conversation, reluctant to leave. I pulled Charles over to where Bob and Elie were still surrounded by a few lingering students and guests of the center. Finally, it was our turn. When Bob introduced me to Elie Wiesel, the rebbe took my hands into his.

Bob told Elie that I was a mother, an activist, and an eager student of his work. Elie said he was pleased to meet me. I didn't say anything. Later, I imagined my sudden voicelessness must have made me look like a silly schoolgirl. But to my credit, I understood the solemnity of the moment of our meeting. The man who still grasped my hands, who had watched his family die, who had heard the cries of the children and entered the night that still has no end, was the spokesperson for six million others.

Elie moved on and Bob followed, but not before he whispered, "You touched him."

Feeling more than a little embarrassed, I wished that I could tell Bob how I was feeling. Having touched him, the connection that I couldn't seem to resist had been confirmed. It could continue now. There was still more for me to learn from Elie Wiesel.

Instead, I laughed and reached out to Bob for a hug. I couldn't help myself; I loved the rebbe, too.

✶ ✶

Only a few days after Elie's talk, I went to visit Jeremy's grave. I knew the marker I had ordered in December had been set by now. It had been nine years since I had come to find him; the only other time was about six weeks after he died. I wandered around the huge cemetery, trying to remember where the children's plots were. After an hour of going in circles, I saw a row of large markers that looked familiar. Behind it would be the infants and children. I tried to find his row, his place. No marker. Suddenly I knew that he should be here. I got down on my hands and knees, searching for a little stone number 62. What had they done with him? A demon inside of me was doubting his existence. His little body in its wooden coffin, had it dissolved to dust so soon? Had they buried another in his grave? Tears fell in the grass as I frantically searched for the place where my son and his name should be.

Eventually, I had to check the cemetery office to be sure. They were very apologetic. The stone had not been set. They would get right on it.

I went back to Jeremy's grave, and I knew. Six million dead, without graves or names, and Elie held them in his heart as a living graveyard. For him, all that was left of the past was an enormous black cloud.

> Forget the cloud? The black cloud which is Grandmother, her son, my mother. What a stupid time we live in! Everything is upside down. The cemeteries are up above, hanging from the sky, instead of being dug in the moist earth.
>
> —Elie Wiesel, The Accident

I remembered the moment I had considered cremating my son, and I thanked God for the wisdom of a grieving grandmother which kept me from such a decision. In her own way, she had understood: The grief could only end if a place could be found for it to begin. How blessed to have a place where I can find more than ashes, where I can touch his name in the stone and know with all certainty that once he was here with me.

# A Child
# at Dawn

*Memory . . . is both a graveyard and a kingdom.
It has been a graveyard; now it can begin to be a kingdom,
opening up a future "whose newness," David confides in us,
"still makes me dizzy." A blessed state. Better than the
equilibrium of despair.*

—Robert McAfee Brown,
*Elie Wiesel: Messenger to All Humanity*

During the last weeks of the course, Elie
Wiesel became my constant companion. I
talked about him often, with Charles, with
little Melissa, now a sensitive eight-year-old, and with just
about anyone who would listen. He became more and more

present once a week when Terry and I met, especially when we spoke about the child who, in spite of all I had remembered, in spite of all I had learned, was still lost to me.

Immersed in the past, I was working hard to find something new, something unexpected that would transform the present. Terry urged me on, firmly and lovingly.

"You must do it, Molly," she would say, her face alive with belief and hope. And so, over and over again, I remembered.

I was surprised at how clear it all was. Images of the week that Jeremy lived and died unfolded before me, unchanged by time, secrets thought to be sealed forever, now being cautiously retold. I studied the mother in the memories and wondered why she had acted the way she did. And then, dismally, I would remember that the mother was me.

Could the past be relived so that it came out differently? I looked to my ally, Elie Wiesel, and I knew the answer. The past would not change because of the remembering.

*It will always be so sad that I allowed myself to be separated from my little boy. It will always be so sad that we did not say good-bye. Who did this terrible thing? Someone must take the blame for the loneliness of a dying child.*

Again the guilt, ravaging the heart and stilling all hopefulness, held me hostage in a story with no ending. There is more, I thought desperately, there must be more that can be told. The pain could not be contained; past and present became one in the darkness. Yet the next step was elusive.

I became determined: I would search for an ending to my story.

*"Look at the sky," Pedro said. "It's getting light. The night's disappearing."*

—Elie Wiesel, *The Town Beyond the Wall*

The newness that I was seeking began, not surprisingly, in the words of Elie Wiesel, in the dark places of his memory, in the night that contains the truth. I remember. I was, for some reason, alone in our house. Curled up in a chair in our living room, I was reading another of Elie's stories, feeling familiar feelings of connection.

As the divine plan of all storytellers would have it, it was in Elie's memory of another mother and another son, who lived long ago, that I saw myself most clearly. It was in her story, and what happened to me when I felt her pain and shared her guilt, that I began to find the transforming grace. It was Elie and his ghosts who were to be my sweet liberators.

Elie called them out, this mother and her son, gently encouraging them to remember. He didn't reveal much about them; when we read Elie Wiesel, we know the setting: the camps, the selection, the screams of separation, the abrupt ending of all hope. As for me, the words he gave them were sufficient. And I knew, finally, that the agony I felt when I read the story of this other mother had never been mine alone:

"I should have rushed forward, gone with him.
He was so small, so far away."
"Try not to think about it anymore," said my Father.
"I can't."
"Make the effort; you must. You can't go on like
this. You have no right to. What you did, others have done.
By accusing yourself, you condemn all the mothers who
did what you did. You are unfair to them."
Her head was tossing on the pillow. "No, no, " she
said. "I did not behave well. I should have understood.
And refused to be separated from my little boy."

*Though awake, she was still following her ghost*
*and her breath was halting.*

—Elie Wiesel, *The Oath*


Yes, that is it! Who would have thought that anyone else could have known?

I sat shivering in my chair, suddenly aware of the stillness of the house.

*Yes, I know how you must have felt. It will never be over. Death happens, intruding into our ordered delusion of forever and ever. Death is the story with a beginning and no end.*

*It was the same with me. My chance has come and gone. We did not say good-bye. He lay dying in his little bed alone. Once in a while, a stranger wearing a mask over her mouth rocked him in a wooden rocking chair. I did not behave well. I should have understood, and refused to be separated from my little boy.*

*My little boy. It is so hard to let go. If only we could be together for one more moment.* Could the wound still be healed, and the sin still forgiven?

For the other mother, in another time and place, the encounter had failed:

> *He comes, looks at me and goes away. I run after*
> *him, but the distance between us does not diminish.*
> *And so I shout, I scream. He stops and so do I. . . .*
> *I begin to shout again, to scream, but he has already*
> *disappeared. He is angry with me, I know that he is angry*
> *with me. I shouted too late.*
>
> —Elie Wiesel, *The Oath*

These haunting words of the storyteller found a fine home in my wounded spirit. Two voices from deep within me pierced the silence, arguing relentlessly.

*It is too late,* one would say.

To which the other would reply, *I cannot give you up. Not yet.*

I slammed the book shut in order to silence all the voices. It was my turn to speak:

*Yes, Elie, you have done well.*

*My fears and weaknesses leap out at me from the pages of your past and the stories of your beloved six million. But your lesson, rebbe, is not just to confront death in the past, but to confront life in the present. And I can be patient, just as you have been. I must be patient. There is a way out of this hell, and its name is love.*

*Every death leaves a scar, and every time*
*a child laughs it starts healing.*

—Elie Wiesel, *The Gates of the Forest*

It was as inevitable as turning to the next page. The mystery of memory, once embraced, gave way to the promise of possibility. The new kingdom, at long last, opened up.

The book was Elie Wiesel's *A Jew Today,* and the passage was called "A Man and His Little Sister." I had read these words several times before. But when on the last day of class my teacher, Elie's good friend, read them aloud to us, they became for me the greatest gift of Elie's memory and imagination. He began:

Will you remember me? Tell me. Will you remember me, too?

*Of course.*

It was a conversation, a quiet little talk between two people who dearly loved each other. They lingered over the memories of the past, so as to speak to each other in the present:

But you will speak even when you do not see me?
*I shall try.*

You will say that I liked to sing? That I liked to listen to you sing?
*I shall say that too.*

And that I loved the Holy Days?
*You radiated joy.*

And Shabbat? You won't forget to say how much I loved Shabbat?
*It made you glow.*

And the Shabbat songs?
*You sang them at the table.*

And you will speak of my love of God?
*Yes, little sister.*

And my grief at losing you, losing all of you, you will speak of that too?
*I shall carry it inside me.*

And finally, they brought forth the memory of a terrible, terrible hurt. Quickly, recognition resounded in my being; instantly I knew those feelings of separation, regret, and grief.

One more thing.
*Yes?*

When you speak of your little sister leaving you like that, without a hug, without a goodbye, without wishing you a good journey, will you say that it was not her fault? *It was not your fault.*

—Elie Wiesel, *A Jew Today*

There we were, Jeremy and I, living inside Elie's memory of his little sister, Tzipora. Was Jeremy Tzipora, or was I? I wanted so much to understand and to hold on to what I recognized in Elie's words. The parting between Elie and his little sister had taken only an instant. It was barely recognizable as the important moment that it was, and later he struggled to recapture it and recreate more of the image than his tortured memory had recorded. The anguish that must have caused him! I, too, suffered for the memory of an instant, and I, too, was searching for the one person who could offer a healing word, and a new ending.

Again and again, over the days that followed, I looked back at this scene. I wanted to clap and shout, and celebrate their victory over death. *You did it! You refused to be separated!* And I think now that my heart knew how close I was to the miracle.

Suddenly, it sounded like a simple task. Jeremy and I must talk.

I envisioned such a moment, and planned for the joy it could bring. A soothing, completing moment, when I would be forever distracted from searching for what couldn't be found, when a new light would penetrate the darkness and change forever my relationship with this one unique pain.

For months, I hoped it would happen. Yet every time I tried, I stopped short of listening for a reply. I prayed for patience; I trembled when I looked for him. And then one day it happened, because Jeremy was the one who began.

# Dialogue between a Son
and His Mother

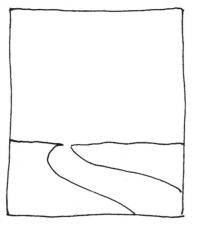

Were you happy when I was born?
*Oh yes. Dad and I were both very happy. We even cried for joy.*

I knew you were happy. I just wanted you to tell me. I remember how they put me on your stomach. They didn't leave me there long enough, though.

*I didn't think it was long enough, either. It was my first time, and I didn't know I could make my own decisions.*

So you remember my first cry?
*Yes.*

And the first time they brought me to you?
*Yes. You were beautiful. You had smooth olive skin and brown hair. You had long fingers like mine.*

Everyone said I looked like Dad. And that was nice. But you know what?

*What?*

I wanted to look like you.

*You did? Why?*

Because you had carried me with you for so long. You were everything to me. I wanted to be just like you.

*I hadn't thought of that.*

What else do you remember, Mother?

*Lots of things. I remember the way your eyes opened and closed and the way your hands moved in your sleep.*

What else?

*I remember the way you breathed and the way you cried.*

What else?

*I remember your little foot sticking out of the blanket. It was so cute.*

And when they undressed me for you?

*I was afraid you might be cold.*

I was. I was so glad to be in your arms. It felt safe and warm.

*You didn't want to eat.*

I'm sorry you were so worried. I could see you frowning, even behind that mask.

*I hated that mask.*

I know, but it didn't matter. I just wanted to be with you.

*I couldn't kiss you through the mask. I don't know why.*

You kissed me with your eyes, Mother. I could feel your eyes loving me, especially the night I took the formula. I could feel your eyes following me down the hallway.
*That was the last time.*

Last time for what?
*The last time I held you. Did you miss me after that?*

Yes. But then I would just remember you.
*Remember me?*

Yes. I remembered how warm your body felt. You protected me for nine months. You gave me life. Then you held me for two days. We could look at each other.
*Yes, we looked at each other.*

You remember? I would close my eyes and imagine you, imagining me.
*I have imagined you often.*

I remember your heart beating. And you would say my name.
*I love that name.*

I remember your blond hair and your green eyes. I remember your smile. I remember your tears. I knew you loved me.
*But I went away.*

Yes, but I could always remember.
*I'm sorry. I never said good-bye.*

Neither did I. I'm sorry too. We didn't know.
*No, we didn't.*

Will you tell them about me?
*Who?*

My sisters and brothers.
*Of course.*

What will you tell them about me?
*Everything.*

Will you tell them I didn't cry very much?
*Yes.*

And that I tried to eat for you?
*Yes.*

And that you will never forget me?
*Neither will they. I will give them my memory of you.*

Listen, Mother, I know what we'll do.
*What's that?*

You tell all those who come after me, and I'll tell all those who came before me.
*What will we tell them?*

How we loved each other.
*I love you, Jeremy.*

I love you, Mother.

# Our Common
# Mourning

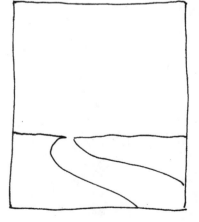

*Suffering confers neither privileges nor rights;*
*it all depends on how one uses it. . . . Neither ends*
*nor means, it can bring him closer to his truth*
*and his humanity.*

—Elie Wiesel, *A Jew Today*

My friend Robert McAfee Brown, upon considering my unlikely liaison with Elie Wiesel, wrote these now-treasured words: "Death, which is no respecter of persons, is no respecter of numbers either. And in death's mysterious mathematics, the pain at the loss of a single child can be infinite, while the pain at the loss of six million lives can be . . . no more than infinite. This does not minimize by one jot or tittle the magnitude of six million deaths; it simply acquaints us more sensitively with the unbelievable magnitude of a single death."

My experience, and the experience of many others whom I have met over the years, was one of infinite pain. For our own sakes, we make this claim. As Bob reminds us, acknowledgment of personal suffering does not ignore the infinite pain of any other loss, but instead removes the illusion of limitation. We feel what we feel—it is beyond us to limit grief.

And again, as with any profound human experience, grief is meant to be shared. *We lead each other* to a safe place to feel, to weep, to begin to laugh again. With this in mind I offer the following as the signposts that marked my way to healing. If you are in need of someone to grieve this very special sorrow with you, I offer myself as a companion. More important, I urge you to share your grief—your anger, guilt, confusion, hopelessness—with others who have walked this ravaged way before you, and with those who love you best.


**I.** HONOR YOUR GRIEF PROCESS
*You have the right to feel, mourn, and be healed.*

Despite all we have learned about grief in the past thirty years, we are still sometimes discouraged from truly mourning a miscarriage, stillborn birth, or even the death of a newborn. Only recently, I heard a woman who had just endured a miscarriage at twenty weeks be told by a well-meaning loved one that "it wasn't meant to be." Other common comforting devices include blaming God's will, citing the blessing that the baby "didn't suffer very much," warning that the child "wouldn't have been right," suggesting that "it was probably better this way," and encouraging the mother to simply "have another baby soon."

These well-intentioned comments are uttered by beloved family members, trusted counselors, and concerned friends. But more often the effect is to minimize the pain you are feeling as the parent. If your loss can be summed up in a single sentiment, why can't your feelings be dismissed in a day or two? In fact, emotions are meant to be felt, lived out, and ultimately transformed as part of our lifelong process of growth. If you feel loss, sorrow, emptiness, or even moments of desolation, you are meant to walk through this valley, supported by the ones who love you. Some of us heal quickly, others with more of a struggle. Whatever the process entails for you, you have a right to claim that passage.

As for words of comfort, suggest that all you need to hear is, "Whatever you're feeling, I'm willing to walk with you."

*Your pain is without comparison.*

Although mourning a miscarriage or the death of a newborn is a different process than mourning the death of a teenager, or a spouse, or a grandmother, or ten strangers with whom we might identify, comparison is useless and deceptive. Failing to appreciate the uniqueness of my pain, I was tempted time after time to devalue my feelings because I understood that others had suffered more.

There is a spectrum of grieving, but that truth has nothing to do with the individual occasion of loss. I have a very close friend, Judy, whose husband and two of her children—half her family—were killed by a drunk driver. Quite clearly, she believes that my understanding of her pain is founded in my own experience of losing a week-old infant. Incredibly, we do share something exquisite—the astonishing event of loss and survival. Certainly, I am humbled by her connection with me, but not only would she never compare our losses, it would never occur to her to set the two side by side in any other way but to honor them both.

*A miscarriage is the most underrated grief experience of the human journey.*

What is the death of a child? It is, indeed, a question mark. It is the loss of hope, of imaginings, of order within the future. It is persistent, stinging regret, a lifetime of "what if"s. The life of a child, however shortened, is still very real to those who have already begun to imagine the future with a new baby and known, as only a happily pregnant woman can, his or her existence within her. It is a life simply unlived, and grief for the loss of that dream can be profound.

Having experienced two miscarriages, I suggest that it is an event capable of provoking deep longing and debilitating emptiness, especially for those who have no other children to offer relief from the pain. Where once life seemed full of hope and promise, only questions remain. What day would he have been born? What would she have been like? What are we missing, now that the baby we created is gone? The reality of motherhood has only begun to blossom when its source is suddenly taken away. Unable to keep up with such profound changes, both body and spirit continue to act as if the hope was still alive; that "feeling" given forth by the life within us persists for a long while after its death.

Grieving for your children lost to miscarriage is appropriate and should be honored. A small ceremony with your loved ones, planting a new tree, time away to befriend the feelings and imagine a new future—all these concrete acts will help. The message is clear—if you are in pain, be kind to yourself. Grieve until you are healed. And enable others to grieve as they must.

*With the new century comes a new dimension to grief.*

Some parents are experiencing a new grief process, one that I could not have imagined during my years of childbearing, one that measures sorrow in a new, more complex mathematics of loss. Especially during the past decade, conception has found a new home—in the offices of infertility experts. Here, success is as wildly glorious as failure is profoundly devastating. Parents sometimes face Solomon-like decisions as embryos are counted, calculated, blessed, or let go. One mother faces the question, "How many can survive?" while another prays for the safekeeping of one. Multiple births risk multiple loss; choosing leaves only question marks in its wake.

And yet, I say this, too, is part of the process of creation. Anyone who brings love to the dream of a child begins the realization of that dream in the best part of our common humanity. In that way, we all share the grief, and the joy, of those who risk great loss in the hope of bearing a child. In the future, there will be many more victories, born of your courage.

**II.** YOU AND YOUR CHILD HAVE A REAL, UNDENIABLE BOND.
*Call each other by name.*

The most important moment of my healing process came when I saw Jeremy's name on his gravestone. "I have another son," I could say then with all certainty. The words marked his reality for me, and offered proof of his existence.

Although we don't have Jeremy's photograph, a friend made us a set of cards with beautiful artwork, his name, the dates of his birth and death, and comforting words that became his alone. Many concrete memorials, whether they be words, a place, or keepsakes will give you a connection to a baby who will always be a part of you.

Even as I claim Jeremy's identity securely now, I find that there is a time and place to acknowledge him publicly. When I am asked how many children I have, I often say, "Six," because I choose not to share my son's story. But a new friend or even an acquaintance will soon know the truth—that I am the mother of seven. It is vitally important for you, especially if you are the mother who carried the child, to take any comfortable opportunity to remember and include him or her as part of your life. Jeremy will always be my son, and I will always be his mother. Sometimes, I need others to know that clearly.

*There are no absolutes.*

The questions facing many of us have been devastating:

Will I find the courage to see and hold my stillborn child? Now that I know my baby is dying, how can I hold her, a daughter I will never see grow up? How will I survive the undeniable attachment to my son and then the terrible letting him go?

I have several friends who chose to spend time with their stillborn infants only after heartfelt support and encouragement from their families, health care professionals, and other parents who assured them that they would not regret this painful decision. My niece brought a tiny blanket to wrap her stillborn son in, took his picture, and held him close to both examine the miracle that he was and say good-bye. She told me that initially the idea of such a moment seemed almost unthinkable, but embraced by a gathering of supporters, she made what she realized later was a healthy and ultimately healing decision.

Even with this evidence, I would never suggest that remembering your stillborn baby in other ways is not appropriate. The important choice is to grieve, to fight denial, and to befriend the emotions, painful as they are. The way to that blessed state is in the heart of each of us.

ᐟ ᐟ

There is surely nothing as devastating as watching your child die. It is a choice I wish I had made. But because there are no absolutes, and despite years of wrestling with my past, I understand that this choice could be impossible. If this was true for you, know that you are not alone.

If you are facing the terrifying possibility of watching your baby die or are the loved one of a parent in this agonizing dilemma, ask for help. Support for the act of accompaniment is now the sole task of a myriad of specially trained health care or hospice women and men. The short life of an infant is infinitely precious, and those who are part of it are infinitely blessed. Later, the memory will become a friend. And there will have been no lost moment for love, and no regrets.

*The reality of another sibling belongs to the whole family.*

Once, when our daughter Melissa was about ten, she came to me in tears. I asked her what was wrong, and she said that she missed Jeremy. "How could this be possible?" she wanted to know. The empty space where Jeremy should have been had become real to her—a void I knew well. When I assured her that her grief was quite possible, she imagined aloud what it would be like to have an older brother. "He would be twelve, and even though we might fight a little, I would have someone older to lean on sometimes, rather than having to be the oldest for all the rest. I would really like that." To mediate their rivalry and celebrate their support of each other—I would have liked that too.

Our six other children are somehow as comforted by the firm acknowledgment of their brother who, for each of them, is "both younger and older than myself." We all claim him to be part of us. He is part of this family's identity, and a precious bond among us.

### III. REMEMBER THE PAST.
*It is never too late.*

*"Do not forget!"* From my friend Elie Wiesel I learned a song of liberation. He helped me find the one I had lost, the child whose memory I buried before I buried him. I had to go back to the beginning, reconstruct the events, call them forth, and accept them willingly. Then I was ready to heal.

Denial becomes an abyss—a trap everything falls through to become entangled in a web of confusion, dishonesty, silence, and limitation. A memory that has been denied is an enemy within us, waiting to show itself. We must allow the film to roll, and dare to watch it.

The time to remember is now. An eighty-year-old friend of mine told me that as she read my story, her arms began to ache. She remembered that when her eleventh child was stillborn forty-six years ago, her arms ached for months afterward, and until now, she never understood why. "They took her away. No one talked about her. But I knew her, and I needed to hold her, just once."

A lifetime later, my friend gave herself permission to grieve. "I have another daughter," she said, and finally took comfort in her memory.

*Save some mercy for yourself.*

Within each of us, often hiding in our unclaimed past, is the most destructive, insidious, and long-lived part of the grief process—guilt. Guilt lies in wait while we search for a place to lay blame. We ask, "Why?" and guilt answers much too quickly.

My husband tried to take the blame for Jeremy's fatal condition the night he said good-bye to him in the hospital. "It's me," he said, referring to the coincidence of heart problems in his family. Even the assurance of genetic counseling left him with lingering doubts.

A friend of mine tried unsuccessfully for years to carry a child to term. After each miscarriage, besides a whole new abyss of loneliness, she was left with the same self-indictment: "What's wrong with me? Why can't I have a healthy child?"

An understandable question with an answer that may seem inadequate: *You are not to blame.* If, in time, it proves to be true your body holds within it barriers to successful child-bearing, it is certainly your personal tragedy to bear, rather than your personal responsibility to accept. Your spirit—the essence of who you are—is utterly blameless, and believing that, you can properly mourn your misfortune.

Unbelievably, the ravages of guilt can be even worse. There are many women who have chosen to have an abortion and then, later in their lives, suffered a miscarriage—perhaps more than one. *An eye for an eye,* the guilt in each woman suggests. The one she wanted in exchange for the one she didn't want. The painful process she went through to make the first choice is forgotten, and her fate reduced to some cruel balance sheet.

I have watched several women suffer through this terrible event, knowing that ultimately they would have to resolve their notions of God, justice, and retribution within themselves. But in the meantime, there are several things that should be said.

Does life work like a balance sheet? My answer is, of course not. It is easy to confuse your losses. Your present grief is tapping into the grief of another loss—one that may never be fully resolved. Grief turned to guilt over a decision that you made in the best way that you could at the time is keeping you from the feelings at hand—the sadness and emptiness of what has befallen you. Save some mercy for yourself. You have a right to mourn what you have lost. And then go on living, and believe that just like the millions of others who have lost a baby to miscarriage, the odds are with you, and you will someday have a child.

*The past will not change.*

A close cousin to guilt is shame. "I did not behave well," said the woman in Elie Wiesel's memory. "I should have understood. And refused to be separated from my little boy." For years, the center of my denial was shame. And when I finally pulled back the curtain hiding the past, I was incredulous. How could I have abandoned my dying child?

Taking responsibility for your actions is important, as is not taking responsibility for the actions of others. Despite all the mitigating factors, I chose to separate from my son, and I cannot go back and do things differently. But I did *not* choose to be encouraged to stay away or to be manipulated into staying away by the very people who should have understood my confusion and vulnerability. Their sin was not showing me a safe way through my fear and into my grief. Their job was to keep Jeremy and me together.

I could not change the past. But I could change my relationship with it. Where once I was ashamed, I am now sad. Where once I ran from the memory of my son, I now hold it dear. Where once I looked for someone to blame, I now offer gentle counsel to those facing the same impossible choices.

*Grief waits for a woman.*

Miscarriage, stillborn birth, or infant death is a terrible loss for a father. And yet, the nature of the grief experienced by a mother is consistently more active, as if it remains alive within her, awaiting moments to show itself and remind her of not only her loss, but the eternal connection she has with her child.

I held that reminder at bay for ten years, while my husband walked headlong into those terrifying feelings when he chose to visit Jeremy in the hospital before he died. This is hard to explain. Was he the stronger of the two of us, or was the loss of the child I had carried inside my body for nine months simply too devastating for me to face? Perhaps both are true. He was stronger because he could be; I turned away because I could not do what was, at the time, impossible.

One of the most powerful emotional displays I've ever witnessed occurred last summer when we attended a family wedding. When we arrived, my seventy-year-old Irish aunt was standing outside the door of the church, sobbing uncontrollably, big red blotches on her pale skin. My uncle stood next to her, hands at his side, expressionless. Other family members formed an uneasy circle around her, obviously embarrassed by what they saw as excessive distress.

But the feelings brought on by the event of the wedding had surprised her, and what reemerged in that moment was the grief of another time. "What's wrong, Aunt Helen?" I said, moving to her side. It took her a moment to speak and even then she only managed a single word, "Mary."

Mary, I remembered, was the name of her third child, her only girl, who died after a few days of life. This wedding—a celebration of joy, a fulfillment of promise—made Helen's sorrow present once again.

Later, after vows had been exchanged and champagne began to flow, we sat together for a while. "I'm sorry, Auntie," I said. "I think I understand."

"Yes," she said, "our children took with them a piece of our hearts. Every once in a while, we remember that something is missing."

Jeremy will always have a piece of my heart. The memory of him still comes back, moving me quickly to tears, suggesting a return to desolation. But I have learned to wait, to allow the feelings to wash over me, and imagine the pain to be a reminder only of my capacity for love. Because I would have loved Jeremy so much better than I could then, if he had stayed with me. I believe he knows that, but it is ultimately more important that I know it.


IV. THERE ARE OTHERS WHO KNOW
HOW YOU FEEL.
*Shared grief is empowerment.*

The most surprising outcome of finally and completely mourning for my son was its connection with something much larger than the two of us. Grief is the most common of all human experiences. Everyone grieves, some more often than others, some more gently than others; some, as my friend Judy says, on a daily basis, when every morning brings the question, "Will I really live today, or will today be a day simply to survive?"

It must be significant that every human being shares the connection of sorrow and loss. The meaning, I believe, is that grief, when lived through, is a path to truth. How many of us say that a devastating loss has changed our lives, sharpened our perspective, humanized our relationships, and transformed our values?

As my final reflection, I offer this as my truth: I am not alone in my grief over a baby boy with brown hair and olive skin, with long fingers that move in his sleep, who asks me to remember him to those who would have loved him. My grief insists on the connectedness of all human suffering. The connection is made not in the death of Jeremy itself, but in the feelings—the sorrow, the guilt, the emptiness—experienced in the ending of an unlived life.

When I met Elie Wiesel, someone who had memorized and multiplied my feelings, I was taught— reminded—of how others have felt. "Re-create the universe," he exalts anyone who has allowed themselves to feel the pain of another. Acts of compassion are, for him, the natural outcome of grieving. Mothers in other times and places have felt what I've felt, and often the caring and intervention of others could have prevented their suffering. Because we share the experience of loss, the cause of their pain becomes part of me, too. I must grow from a concerned bystander to an empowered companion. I must seize this gift, my own heightened humanity, and take it to a suffering world. In fact, we must insist on connecting with other parents who suffer, who have lost children to hunger, violence, war, and inhumanity—a daring, stubborn insistence upon remaining human in the face of evil, and of finding one another, despite separation.

But first, we mourn. Grieving becomes healing. Healing leads to empathy, which suggests bold acts of compassion. When we, together, transform our grief into compassion, then we claim a small role in the story—yet to be told—of the re-creation of the universe. Grief and compassion. The question mark, and the answer.

# Acknowledgments

My sincerest thanks and love to my friends and family, for their unending support.

My special gratitude to Terry Johnston, Bob Brown, and Judy Peckler for making the connections with me; to Melissa, Mark, Nicholas, Gino, Kristen, and Joel Fumia for their patience; to Helen Menden for the gift of time; and to Tom Gumbleton for being on my side.

My deepest appreciation to Frank J. Cunningham of Ave Maria Press, and to the amazing group at Conari Press, who just keep believing. And finally, to Mary Jane Ryan, who lovingly named my profession, and has walked with me through just about everything

# Resource Guide

**ASIP: Association of SIDS and Infant Mortality Programs**
Minnesota SID Center
2525 Chicago Avenue South
Minneapolis, Minnesota 55404
621-813-6285

**Center for Infant and Child Loss**
630 West Fayette Street, Room 5-684
Baltimore, Maryland 21201-1585
410-706-5062

**CLIMB: Center for Loss in Multiple Births**
P. O. Box 91377
Palmer, Alaska 99509
907-222-5321
Web site: www.climb-support.org
e-mail: climb@pobox.alaska.net

**The Compassionate Friends, Inc.**
P. O. Box 3696
Oak Brook, Illinois 60522-3696
630-990-0010

**HAND: Helping After Neonatal Death**
P. O. Box 341
Los Gatos, California 95031
800-963-7070

**The National SIDS Resource Center**
2070 Chain Bridge Road, Suite 450
Vienna, Virginia. 22182
703-821-8955
Web site: www.circsol.com/sids
e-mail: sids@circsol.com

**Pregnancy and Infant Loss Center, Inc.**
1421 East Wayzata Boulevard, Suite 70
Wayzata, Minnesota 55391
612-473-9372

**SHARE: Pregnancy and Infant Loss Support, Inc.**
300 First Capitol Drive
St. Charles, Missouri 63301
800-821-6819

**Sudden Infant Death Syndrome Alliance**
1314 Bedford Avenue, Suite 210
Baltimore, Maryland 21208
800-221-SIDS

**The Tenderhearts Support-Triplett Connection**
P. O. Box 99571
Stockton, California95209
209-474-0885

## BOOKS

If you want to read further, consider:

Davis, Deborah. *Empty Cradle, Broken Heart.* Golden, CO:
    Fulcrum, 1996.
Finkbeiner, Ann. *After the Death of a Child: Living with Loss
    through the Years.* Baltimore, MD: John Hopkins
    University Press, 1998.
Isle, Sherokee. *Empty Arms: Coping with Miscarriage,
    Stillbirth, and Infant Death.* Itasca, IL: Wintergreen
    Press, 1992.
Kluge-Bell, Kim. *Unspeakable Losses: Understanding the
    Experience of Pregnancy Loss, Miscarriage and Abortion.*
    New York: W. W. Norton & Co., 1998.
Lafser, Christine O'Keeffe. *An Empty Cradle, A Full Heart:
    Reflections for Mothers and Fathers after Miscarriage,
    Stillbirth, or Infant Death.* Chicago: Loyola, 1998.
Lanham, Carol Cirulli. *Pregnancy after Loss: A Guide to
    Pregnancy after Miscarriage, Stillbirth, or Infant Death.*
    New York: Berkley Publishing Group, 1999.

## CATALOGS

**Answering Life's Challenges**
Colorado Springs, Colorado
719-593-0957

**Centering Corporation**
Omaha, Nebraska
402-553-1200

**Compassion Books**
Burnsville, North Carolina
828-675-5909

**Courage to Change**
Arlington, Virginia
703-276-0800

**Hazelden Educational Materials**
Center City, Minnesota
651-257-4010

**Quiescence**
Cushing, Maine
207-354-9264


## ONLINE RESOURCES

**www.bu.edu/cohis/teenpreg/neohlth/stillborn.htm**
What stillbirth is, how you might feel, what you might
see, and what its causes are.

**www.ivf.com**
Diary of a woman who suffered a miscarriage.

**www.sandswa.org.au**

Support group for parents who experience miscarriage, stillbirth, or neonatal death.

**www.shareatlanta.org**

Perspectives, poetry, letters, diary entries, and stories about grieving for neonatal death, miscarriage, and stillbirth to help parents endure the grief and to advise others who want to support parents.

# References

The following books by Elie Wiesel have been quoted in the text. The original titles in French and publication dates are in parentheses.

*The Accident* (*Le Jour*, 1961). New York: Bantam Books, 1982.

*Ani Maamin, A Song Lost and Found Again*. New York: Random House, 1974. Bilingual edition.

*A Beggar in Jerusalem* (*Le Mendiant de Jerusalem*, 1968). New York: Random House, 1970.

*The Gates of the Forest* (*Les Portes de la Forêt*, 1964). Austin, TX: Holt, Rinehart and Winston, 1966.

*A Jew Today* (*Un Juif Aujourd'hui*, 1978). New York: Vintage Books, 1979.

*Night* (*La Nuit*, 1958). New York: Bantam Books, 1982.

*The Oath* (*Le Serment de Kolvillag*, 1973). New York: Avon Books, 1973.

*Souls on Fire* (*Célébration Hassidique,* 1972). New York:
Vintage Books, 1972.

*The Town Beyond the Wall* (*La Ville de la Chance,*1962).
Austin: TX: Holt, Rinehart and Winston, 1964.

"Why I Write." In *Confronting the Holocaust: The Impact of
Elie Wiesel.* Edited by Alvin H. Rosenfeld and Irving
Greenberg. Bloomington, IN: Indiana University Press,
1978.

Also quoted:

Robert McAfee Brown. *Elie Wiesel: Messenger to All Humanity.*
Notre Dame, IN: University of Notre Dame Press,
1983.

# To Our Readers

ONARI PRESS publishes books on topics ranging from spirituality, personal growth, and relationships to women's issues, parenting, and social issues. Our mission is to publish quality books that will make a difference in people's lives—how we feel about ourselves and how we relate to one another. We value integrity, compassion, and receptivity, both in the books we publish and in the way we do business.

As a member of the community, we sponsor the Random Acts of Kindness™ Foundation, the guiding force behind Random Acts of Kindness™ Week. We donate our damaged books to nonprofit organizations, dedicate a portion of our proceeds from certain books to charitable causes, and continually look for new ways to use natural resources as wisely as possible.

Our readers are our most important resource, and we value your input, suggestions, and ideas about what you would like to see published. Please feel free to contact us, to request our latest book catalog, or to be added to our mailing list.

2550 Ninth Street, Suite 101
Berkeley, California 94710-2551
800-685-9595     510-649-7175
fax: 510-649-7190     e-mail: conari@conari.com
http://www.conari.com